D0721179

Secure Cloud Transformation: The CIO's Journey

Richard Stiennon

IT-Harvest Press
Birmingham, Michigan

ISBN 13 Paperback: 978-1-945254-20-8
ISBN 13 Hardcover: 978-1-945254-21-5
Copyright © 2019 by IT-Harvest Press, an imprint of IT-Harvest, LLC,
Birmingham, Michigan, USA
www.ith-press.com
All rights reserved.

No part of this book may be reproduced in any form or by any electronic or mechanical
means, including information storage and retrieval systems, without written permission
from the author, except for the use of brief quotations in a book review. All trademarks
referenced are the property of their respective owners.

Table of Contents

Contributing IT Leaders

NAME	COMPANY	SECTOR	PAGE
Philip Armstrong CIO	Great-West Life	Financial Services	222
Ken Athanasiou VP & CISO	AutoNation	Retail	101
Larry Biagini Former VP & CTO	General Electric Company	Conglomerate	205
Hervé Coureil CDO	Schneider Electric	Listed Company	41
Joe Drouin CIO	PulteGroup	Home Construction	245
Tony Fergusson IT Infrastructure Architect	MAN Energy Solutions	Manufacturing	114
Jim Fowler Former Group CIO	General Electric Company	Conglomerate	18
Scott Guthrie EVP, Cloud & Enterprise Group	Microsoft	Cloud Services	171
Frederik Janssen Global Head of Service Portfolio & Lifecycle Management, IT Infrastructure	Siemens	Conglomerate	68
Erik Klein Infrastructure Architect	FrieslandCampina	Dairy	51
Bruce Lee Former CIO	Fannie Mae	Financial Services	233
Stephen Orban General Manager	Amazon Web Services	Cloud Services	181

Introduction

Every time I read an analyst report or speak with the C-Suite on the digitization of enterprise IT and the role of the CIO today, I'm left with this thought—the evidence for this tectonic shift in businesses today is staggering, and yet there isn't a single anthology of real-world testimonials from their peers to help guide CIOs as they embark on this journey.

After a multitude of discussions with several industry leaders and enterprise CIOs, the concept for this book, a real-world collection of best practices for secure digital transformation, was born. This book captures the stories of more than a dozen pioneers in enterprise digital transformation as told by CIOs, CTOs, and CISOs of many Fortune 500 companies. They come from a broad swath of industry including Fannie Mae, Siemens, Microsoft, and General Electric.

From these innovators' stories a common thread emerges, one of early discovery of how digitization and a move to the cloud provides distinct advantages, be they financial or in extending capabilities through greater IT agility, a faster pace of innovation, and lower costs. This shift to the cloud leads to competitive and financial gains for all of the IT visionaries you will find in this book.

TRANSFORMATION JOURNEY

Chapter 1: Mega-Trends Drive Transformation

This chapter highlights the changes that are driving digital transformation, its scope, what it entails, how it transcends the entire value chain and the mega-trends driving this evolution.

Chapter 2: Moving Applications to the Cloud

Here, we address the first stage in enterprise digital transformation cloud-enabled applications; and how applications are moving from enterprise data centers to SaaS (software as a service) or public clouds.

Chapter 3: From Hub-and-Spoke to Hybrid Networks

This chapter focuses on the cloud-enabled network. As business applications move to the cloud, the legacy hub-and-spoke network architecture needs to evolve to support this new environment; decoupling network access from application access, driving cost savings and improving productivity.

Chapter 4: Security Transformation

A deep dive on securing the enterprise transformation to the cloud; highlights best practices to deliver fast and secure user experiences as applications move to the cloud and users become increasingly mobile and distributed.

CHAPTER 1

Mega-Trends Drive Digital Transformation

"Digital transformation goes well beyond technology to our customer experience, our user experience, and business in general. Last year, we created a digital team that would help us in that digital transformation journey. We took into account sales support, automation, and other projects."

Hervé Coureil, Chief Digital Officer, Schneider Electric

Cloud and mobility create opportunities for growth

Organizations are undergoing a massive shift in their IT strategies. The adoption of cloud applications and infrastructure, the explosion of internet traffic volumes, and the shift to mobile-first computing have enhanced business agility and become a strategic imperative for CIOs. Organizations are embracing these trends to empower business users, increase speed of deployment, create new customer experiences, reengineer business processes, and find new opportunities for growth.

Always on, always connected, and always working has become the new mantra for business. Enabling the same direct-to-cloud experience for mobile employees becomes the logical next step for IT. Today, every user is a power user and should be given direct access to corporate data and applications regardless of where they are—at home, at a coffee shop, at a hotel, or on an airplane.

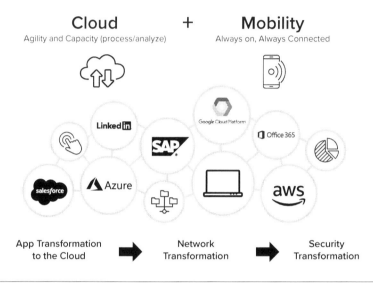

Figure 1.1 Digital transformation drivers

Mega-trends introduce new challenges for enterprises

The convergence of these new trends creates an infinite number of opportunities for innovation and growth. At the same time, it is difficult for enterprises to embrace these trends with the traditional security architectures because it introduces several key IT challenges:

- **Growing use of the cloud and the internet creates gaps in security coverage**. Enterprise applications are increasingly moving from being hosted in on-premises data centers within the corporate network to SaaS applications hosted in the public cloud. The growing use of the public cloud can significantly increase business risk, as security policies that are consistently applied within the traditional corporate network either cannot be enforced or are easily circumvented in a cloud environment.

- **Microsoft Office 365 strains network capacity and data center infrastructure.** Unlike other SaaS applications that are used intermittently or by specific departments, Microsoft Office 365 moves many of an organization's most heavily used applications, such as Exchange and SharePoint, to the cloud, which dramatically increases internet traffic and can potentially overwhelm the existing network and security infrastructure.

- **Workforce mobility makes every user a potential source of security vulnerability.** The shift towards an increasingly mobile workforce has caused employees to demand easy and fast access to the internet as well as on-premises and cloud applications, regardless of device or location. To permit access for their mobile employees, organizations have typically relied on VPNs (Virtual Private Networks), which grant the user access to the corporate network instead of just the application that is requested. This creates increased points of vulnerability, because a single compromised VPN user can expose the entire corporate network.

These challenges are exacerbated by an increasingly severe cyber threatscape

Today's sophisticated hackers, motivated by financial, criminal and terrorist objectives, are exploiting the gaps left by existing network security approaches with increasingly sophisticated and evolving threats. The growing dependence on the internet has increased exposure to malicious or compromised websites. According to Mozilla Firefox, over 50% of browser-based internet traffic is encrypted.[1] Encryption has become one of the most effective tactics

---

1   Half the web is now encrypted. That makes everyone safer. https://www.wired.com/2017/01/half-web-now-encrypted-makes-everyone-safer/

used by hackers to avoid detection by existing appliances. As a result, organizations are more exposed than ever to today's cyberattacks.

The enterprise now needs to rethink how it protects and secures its most valuable assets—its employees, customers, and partners—from ever-rising breaches and cyberattacks.

Application Transformation

Organizations are increasingly relying on internet destinations for a range of business activities, adopting new external SaaS applications for critical business functions and moving their internally managed line-of-business applications to the public cloud, or IaaS (infrastructure as a service). For fast and secure access to the internet and applications, enterprises need to be able to securely migrate their applications from the corporate data centers to the cloud, and from their legacy network architectures to modern direct-to-cloud architectures.

This requires a transformation at the application level whereby policies can be set by the organization to securely connect the right user to the right application, regardless of the device, location, or network they are on:

- Users should be able to securely connect to externally managed applications, including SaaS applications and internet destinations.

- At the same time, authorized users should also have secure and fast access to the internally managed applications hosted in enterprise data centers or the public cloud.

Network Transformation

Enabling fast and secure access to applications and services on the user's device of choice, whether in the cloud or the data center, regardless of where the user is located, demands a shift in thinking—one that requires a change in the way enterprises view their network topology. As the use of cloud drives up the percentage of corporate traffic that is destined for the internet, it becomes obvious that traditional hub-and-spoke network topologies, where traffic is backhauled from remote offices and mobile employees to the data center before reaching the cloud, is no longer optimal. Why backhaul traffic from hundreds of remote offices to headquarters or the data center before sending it on its way to Office 365? This would be analogous to flying from New York to London via Miami! One CTO measures over 100 terabytes of traffic a month to Office 365 alone.

To mitigate this, companies are engaging in "local internet breakouts" as a critical component of their cloud adoption. The concept is simple: each remote location, instead of connecting back to the data center via expensive MPLS (Multiprotocol Label Switching) circuits, has one or more connections to the internet so that the traffic destined to the internet can be peeled off at the source. This is often called network transformation.

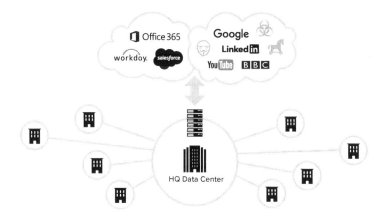

Figure 1.2 Hub-and-spoke network topology

Security Transformation

Because of these application and network transformations, there are security concerns that have had to be addressed along the way. Where data is stored and how it's secured and accessed are much broader security concerns for cloud adoption. With regards to local internet breakouts, traffic was traditionally backhauled because security controls were anchored in the data center to protect the network. In the new world where traffic is going direct-to-cloud over the internet, you don't control the network and network security becomes increasingly irrelevant. And in the new direct-to-cloud world, security needs to move to the cloud.

Cloud transformation has led to a re-architecting of security that is disrupting the security industry itself. Not only are these changes creating challenges for the IT department, but threat actors are evolving too. Hackers are beginning to understand underlying business processes and to target the vulnerabilities in money flows and data stores. A new security approach to protect users and applications is needed.

Three areas of secure cloud transformation

As we will learn from the real-world CxO stories shared throughout this book, there are three phases to secure cloud transformation as illustrated in Figure 1.3 below:

- **Application transformation:** Moving applications to the cloud;

- **Network transformation:** Evolving from a hub-and-spoke topology to hybrid networks;

- **Security transformation:** Securely connecting users and devices to their applications regardless of the network they are on.

It started with cloud application adoption...

Old World

Data Center

Cloud World

Cloud + Data Center

And that drives network transformation...

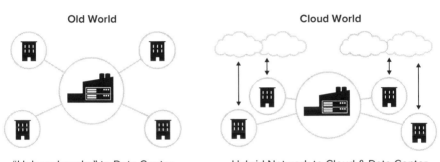

Old World

"Hub-and-spoke" to Data Center

Cloud World

Hybrid Network to Cloud & Data Center

Which disrupts network security

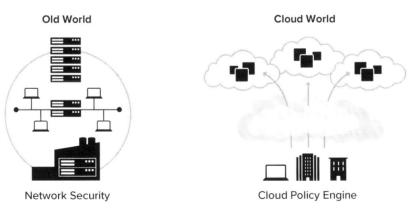

Old World

Network Security

Cloud World

Cloud Policy Engine

Figure 1.3 The three phases of secure cloud transformation

CIO JOURNEY

General Electric Company

Powering Global IT Transformation

Company:	**General Electric**	Revenue:	**$122 billion**
Sector:	**Conglomerate**	Employees:	**300,000**
Driver:	**Jim Fowler**	Countries:	**170**
Role:	**Former CIO**	Locations:	**8,000**

Company IT Footprint: General Electric is a global name and has been an icon of technology innovation for well over a century. At the time of writing, there were about 9,000 IT employees and another 15,000 contractors at GE. They maintained an application portfolio of around 8,000 applications, and were distributed across 45,000 compute nodes. Their IT infrastructure was spread across 300,000 employees who sat in 170 countries around the world.

"We had a target to take a billion dollars of technology costs out of our own operations. And we did it! By the end of 2017, we exceeded the billion dollars of productivity, and we figured out how to deliver three billion dollars' worth of productivity within the same time frame."

Jim Fowler, Former Chief Information Officer, General Electric Company

---

General Electric Company (GE) embraced cloud transformation to improve employee productivity while enabling growth, to reduce the complexity and associated costs of their infrastructure, and to ultimately improve the security posture for mobile users. Here is the story of how GE executed their cloud transformation across 8000 global locations.

In the words of Jim Fowler:

I was the group CIO for General Electric until late 2018 and have been with GE for 18 years, having worked in every one of our businesses (apart from our healthcare business) in that time. I've done everything from being a systems administrator to a Six Sigma Black Belt focused on process excellence and improvement. Around 2015, I was approached for this CIO position where they said, "Hey, we're entering into a time of digital transformation. How we run as a company is going to change drastically as we become technically focused. We'd like you to take this job." This was a significant milestone for us as a company, as none of my predecessors came from IT. They came either from finance or business development. So, I'm the first CIO who has come up from technology inside GE.

The launch of the GE digital software business

Seven years ago, at a request from our CEO, we started looking at what it would take to create a digital software business inside GE. We weren't thinking about GE internally, but instead about creating software to help our customers get more out of the assets that they run. As we went down that path, we started conceptualizing what a GE software business would look like, and we soon realized, You know what? If we're going to look at how we help our customers be more digitally integrated into the systems that they run, we better think about how we do the same thing inside our own four walls. And so, we set a target for ourselves: we would find a way to drive out a billion dollars, cumulative, of productivity cost by using technology that we apply inside GE.

We had a target to take a billion dollars of technology costs out of our own operations. And we did it! By the end of 2017, we exceeded the billion dollars of productivity, and we figured out how to deliver three billion dollars' worth of productivity within the same time frame. We became our own best example of what good digital industry looks like.

A new focus on cloud

The transition to the cloud became important as we realized it was going to take an investment to replicate what we had on-premises in the cloud, and our existing application infrastructure needed to be a lot nimbler. We needed to be able to make changes quickly and spend our resources on application content development rather than infrastructure work like storage and servers.

It started with data center transformation

At that point we had seven data centers around the world that we were housing with our own infrastructure, so we thought: What if we could take the majority of the resources that were in those data centers and get those to be cloud-based? We realized that using the cloud would help us free up the manpower that we needed to drive this new transformational idea.

The cloud strategy we developed was about taking out our own infrastructure from the data center perspective and building upon the idea of reuse versus reinvention. In a cloud-based world, there is a common code set and a common set of software. So we used shared micro-services and common components that allowed us to build applications faster.

In the end, we realized it wasn't just about freeing up resources. It was about increasing the velocity with which we could build our own code. For every dollar we spend in this "world of the cloud," we reuse what we already have, and we see a three- to four-dollar greater return. And that is why our evolution into the cloud has become so important to us.

Next, we needed to transform our workforce

Shifting to the cloud meant replacing our outsourced contractors since we had given up a lot of our expertise in hands-on technology over to third parties. We knew that had to change, so for the last two years, 95% of our new hires have been in entry-level positions. In the last twelve months alone, we've brought in about 1,500 people in a range of new positions—building code, system administration, database administration, and cloud architecture.

Next, we had to focus on our project managers. They knew how to manage outsourced labor, but they needed development on how to run a product. So, we had to build on their product management skills within the current generation of project managers. They had to understand not just how to run a project plan, but also how to manage product development—pricing a product, understanding cost, and how to make investment decisions on features and functions. It was a big transition for them to learn ways to determine output from the company's perspective.

We established guard rails to support innovation

Culturally, I would say one of the hardest things to adapt to has been this idea of reuse versus reinvent. We have a 125-year history full of strong innovation and smart engineers. That culture manifests itself as employees trying to reinvent what somebody else has already done because they think they can do it better.

What they don't realize is that this approach inevitably slows progress, because it takes longer to get to a final solution. We're trying to focus on improving ideas, rather than inventing new ones or reinventing old ones.

In the past year, we've tried to encourage this new focus by implementing what we call a set of guardrails. The guardrails set a minimum standard by which all our developers must operate. But within those guardrails, we welcome and encourage innovation. We like for our people to find newer and better ways to use technology. But when they want to go outside of those guardrails, it requires our chief architects to make an architectural decision to change the guardrails.

Moving towards data protection based on risk tolerance

Changing our network infrastructure was not as hard as we anticipated. We already had a complex network structure because we have over 8,000 different locations that we support. So, instead, we had to focus on data. How do we think about the value of data or the risk of data loss or data manipulation? The answer: we built a data infrastructure on top of the network that protects us from a risk perspective.

For example, we think one percent of our data represents 80% of the risk to the company, and that data sits inside a super-controlled vault of information that is separate from what we consider the rest of the GE network.

We have different classifications of data that determine the level of the network data can reside on from a risk perspective. And once we had that laid out, the networking was really just about a physical design that fit those data requirements. And so, what I always tell people is, don't worry so much about designing the network first. Design your risk tolerance, first as it relates to the loss or manipulation of data, and that will allow you to define how you think about the network in what is going to be a hybrid cloud environment.

Moving from hub-and-spoke to a local internet break-out architectures

We have different types of networks. You'll find our large sites are still using hub-and-spoke networks that come back into a core network architecture that allows connectivity both inside the GE network and out to the GE cloud.

In our smaller locations, we're disconnecting them from the MPLS networks, and we're using local internet providers, like Time Warner or Xfinity in the United States, or Orange in Europe, to provide connectivity to the internet. This allows those small sites to be internet-connected back into the GE world, whether that be a cloud-based solution or an internal GE network.

We think of our smaller sites the same way we think about a home office, where it's internet-connected, and we provide functionality they need. This way the smaller sites can have a secure connection for data and we can manage GE data that sits on the devices in those remote locations rather than try to think about implementing security around the distributed network.

Security is about data, not the network

Our security starts and ends with the definition of the data. We have a strong understanding of the regulatory requirements around how that data is managed. Then we build the enterprise architecture or the physical architecture around that data. So, we design security in from the very beginning of a project based on those discussions. We don't think about security as a set of requirements or checkboxes. We think about security as features that we designed into the product based on decisions around the data.

We also set guidelines on the secure software development lifecycle that require product managers to include security features based on the data requirements and the transactional data that sits in those systems. Then we build an infrastructure around being able to watch and manage how that data moves over time, based on its criticality.

On the network or off: blurring the lines

Our last CTO Larry Biagini predicted that the lines between what's inside the GE network and outside the GE network would blur, making it harder to decipher what is inside the corporate network and what is out the network. Zscaler's cloud security platform provided us a way to think about how to control data in transit in a world where we didn't control the network.

"In the past, we were big VPN users, but have decreased our VPN usage by almost 90% since we started this project."

As a result, we don't run traditional VPN inside GE anymore. We have a custom-built application, which is built on top of some of the Zscaler connectivity that runs on every device. When you connect to any network anywhere in the world, it determines a) are you on something we control or not and b) does your PC have the level of controls on it that we need to protect our data? If not, let's put them there, and if yes, then I'm going to give you access to a certain level of information inside the organization.

What's behind all that is a Zscaler infrastructure that helps us not worry about where somebody might show up to work one day, and it creates that ubiquitous connection between the GE infrastructure and the end user's PC, while enforcing controls. You can control everything from traditional proxy blocking to starting to build intelligence that says, when Jim Fowler shows up on a PC and is sitting in Atlanta, Georgia, giving him access to these network resources makes sense. But when Jim Fowler shows up with his PC in some country we have concerns with, we're going to have to restrict his access a little bit more. We're not necessarily going to give him access, and we're going to monitor more closely what he's doing on that device today. And so Zscaler fills a lot of different boxes—it's not just your traditional proxy provider, but a next-gen network security provider for us. It allows us to manage this extended network of devices that sits out in the GE infrastructure.

In the past, we were big VPN users, but have decreased our VPN usage by almost 90% since we started this project. We are connecting about 3,000 of our smaller locations through a local internet provider versus a high-cost MPLS or dedicated network as we would have had in the past.

In data centers and large locations, we still have dedicated infrastructure, but it's that small office-type location that we think about very differently than we did ten years ago.

Realizing cost savings and performance improvement

Depending on which country the site is in, we see savings from 30% to 75% in infrastructure costs. This comes from being able to leverage more ubiquitous forms of connecting to the internet versus having dedicated lines and firewalls and routers and switches in those locations.

One of the advantages that we weren't looking for, but that we gained, was in performance. In the old world, every transaction routed back through a central data center and then was sent back out to the receiving system. In the new world, when we're connecting via the internet, all of a sudden that network performance goes up. So, wherever we're using cloud-based solutions, we've seen performance improvements with a lot of our transactional applications—as high as 70% improvement in transaction times.

When you break down the barriers of everything having to sit in your own network in your own data center it becomes a lot easier to have conversations with

"Wherever we're using cloud-based solutions, we've seen performance improvements."

customers. About not just how you do that, but also about making the data flow in a secure fashion, so that from a point-to-point perspective, the data is completely secure. Between two different companies, we could actually share data in a more meaningful way than we had in the past. And so, I'd say that lower cost and improved performance were the two big things that we experienced as we went on this journey.

Cloud Security Alliance

Best Practices for Providing Security Assurance
Within Cloud Computing

Organization: **Cloud Security Alliance**   Type: **Non-profit**
Driver: **Jim Reavis**   Role: **Co-founder, CEO**

Organization profile: The Cloud Security Alliance (CSA) is a not-for-profit organization with a mission to promote the use of best practices for providing security assurance within cloud computing, and provide education on the uses of cloud computing to help secure all other forms of computing. CSA harnesses the subject matter expertise of industry practitioners, associations, governments, and its corporate and individual members to offer cloud security-specific research, education, certification, events, and products.

"The need for regulatory compliance probably comes up first for organizations moving to the cloud."

Jim Reavis, Co-founder & Chief Executive Officer, Cloud Security Alliance

---

Cloud Security Alliance (CSA) was created in 2008 to get ahead of the security issues they saw coming with the move to the cloud. Jim Reavis, the co-founder and CEO of CSA, shares in this upcoming journey what motivated the formation of this alliance in the early days of cloud adoption, and also the initiatives the alliance continues to drive to create governance and the sharing of best practices within the community and industry.

In the words of Jim Reavis:

In 2008, I was looking for things that were going to impact the IT industry, like virtualization of operating systems. That's when I started to see that the early adopters I respected were beginning to kick the tires of this thing called cloud.

It became apparent that we were moving to a world where someone armed with a credit card could get access to tremendous computing power to quickly mashup impactful applications.

The problem I anticipated by 2013 was that there would be a lot of cloud options available, but from a security perspective, there would not be a lot of defensible best practices and strategies for cloud adoption, and for understanding the risks in a way that could be communicated to auditors.

This line of thinking started a snowball effect, and after talking to my CISO friends, I realized we really needed to get started on creating a whole cloud security ecosystem.

In 2008, during the financial meltdown, we brought together a group of smart industry people and started creating white papers. We wanted to start from what we understood the cloud was right then, and where it could go. I took these ideas to a group of industry experts from eBay, Intuit, Qualys, and Zscaler. They provided encouragement and access to their networks to find the resources for all the different areas. And then we went to work on it and, at the RSA Conference on April 21, 2009, we announced the Cloud

Security Alliance, with a mission to promote the use of best practices for providing security assurance within cloud computing. We also published *Guidance for Critical Areas of Focus in Cloud Computing* to set the stage for what the CSA was all about.

It took a lot of people by surprise because they were thinking about the need for the same type of organization. But we put together a pretty complete version 1.0 of our *Guidance*. And many of those principles are still in the many iterations we've done since then. From that point on, we were viewed as an authoritative source.

In 2013, we heard a lot of enterprises tell us that having tools like the Guidance saved millions in IT costs, and how they could make the jump to the cloud sooner, because we had some defensible, vendor-neutral, intellectual tools to help explain to the rest of the ecosystem what we were doing.

It was a community, grassroots effort—a coalition of the willing—that just happened to have more time than they normally would have in that 2008 timeframe. From there, we built on the initial success.

At the CSA, we have a philosophy of making all of our research freely available. Sometimes we don't even know how enterprises are using what we do or how they're interacting with it. We see things from a lot of different levels. For example, a large oil and gas company viewed the cloud from a lens of four main pillars: awareness, visibility, opportunism, and strategy. You are already in the cloud. Most places find they are probably using more cloud than they know.

From credit card projects to the entertainment industry, there are small firms that do everything in the cloud. It's an important part of the supply chain, but they also may not necessarily have the same technical visibility as a larger company.

So, understanding why people are using the cloud, what they're using, what problems they're trying to solve, how they're trying to transform the business—it's all key to understanding the impact.

As for *opportunism*, it's important to know it's going to be all cloud in the future in terms of backend data centers. Understanding that, we can find the best ways to move forward on a case-by-case basis, and to use security to solve business problems.

Cloud strategy

Many organizations have settled on a cloud-first strategy. Even the U.S. Federal Government announced in 2011 that it would have a cloud-first strategy.

Strategy is about how to create the organization, technical architecture, culture, communications, and platform. We need to make it much more simple to enable different parts of the business to have what I call a cloud dial-tone.

If you have the right identity federation, and the right policies in place, you can do it your own way.

"Even the U.S. Federal Government announced in 2011 that it would have a cloud-first strategy."

The cloud security landscape

The need for regulatory compliance probably comes up first for organizations moving to the cloud. The data sovereignty and data protection aspects of it are of particular concern because you don't necessarily have control of your own data. If you have a global utility that's overlaid on multiple nation-states with their own regulatory regimes, that makes data sovereignty a paramount issue.

From a technical security perspective, the raw security concerns I see have become more nuanced. We hear from a lot of enterprises that top-tier providers do get it now. They have matured quickly and because of the scope of their platforms, they have visibility into attacks globally.

Cloud service providers have a security responsibility and enterprises need to be able to vet them properly. They need to understand that the cloud isn't just the top five infrastructure providers, but it's thousands of other entities that provide services on top of the infrastructure.

CSA engagement

More than any other sector, the financial services sector is participating heavily in the Cloud Security Alliance. This sector tends to be more sophisticated when it comes to IT. They engage with us more directly and want to share best practices and share their pain points with their peers.

We receive many requests to engage with governments on behalf of our members—engage with regulators and provide the sort of vendor-neutral voice to help them understand what we see. We have to explain what the cloud is, where the risks are, and what they need to be thinking about.

It's exciting times as organizations are trying to become more agile, to be "software-defined" in many aspects of their business.

Identity and federation

With identity and federation, there has been enormous progress. There isn't as much pain involved in being able to take any new application and have the right way to plug that in with SAML (Security Assertion Markup Language) and other federation schemes.

We haven't moved as quickly as I had hoped in having pervasive, multi-factor authentication (MFA) everywhere, but it's certainly in a lot of places, and it's certainly well understood. Going forward, MFA should extend beyond the idea of the human and the user to make sure that anything that's an entity, any internet of things (IoT) device, any virtual machine instance, any data store, any application—anything that you can think of that's a part of this infrastructure—will have an identity. It will have certificates. It will have the ability for us to understand it as a discrete and trusted component so that we can pull things out of it, and we can build a continuous audit trail or whatever else we need based on identity.

Impact on workforce

A big issue we hear about is the retooling of the workforce. Unless you go with some different definition, no one has 20 years' experience in cloud, and so Global 2000 companies are hiring people fresh out of college and training them. You can't run your IT organization on newly minted college graduates, but you need a strong infusion of fresh talent.

At the major cloud provider conferences like AWS re:Invent and some of the others, attendees get excited and charged up about what's possible. It is creating a hunger—but, it's a lot harder to flip a switch on people than it is on systems. It's a slog to get people to change. The work is not all in retraining. We need more bite-sized education on how to do this, across the board, for every role in IT.

Better security through automation

Automation has created a different approach to security. The ability to instantiate and decommission compute, virtual machines, or containers can shrink your attack surfaces. Systems don't degrade with time and vulnerabilities have a much shorter half-life. The traditional ways of very carefully curating servers, like a thoroughbred, are over. Slow regression testing for understanding changes gets replaced by rapid instantiation and decommissioning of systems.

The ability to use automation tools to deploy pristine images decreases the opportunity for vulnerable systems to be attacked. It is so much better than we've ever had before.

What not to do on your cloud journey

It's a new world. Don't take all of your old approaches with you. The other aspect of all this is that it's really cloud-native. You can't assume that there's any physical choke point that's bringing everything back to a corporate enterprise perimeter and analyzing things. You have to understand what a true virtual, cloud-native architecture looks like. When you understand that, you can understand how to move to the cloud securely.

Chapter 1 Takeaways

In this chapter we covered the mega-trends that are driving enterprise digital transformation, the emergence of cloud transformation, and some common considerations. At this stage, you should start thinking about the cloud as your data center, or at least a flexible extension of your data center.

In the next section of this book, we will delve deeper into the transformation journey and glean insights from other enterprise IT leaders and their real-world cloud transformation journeys.

CHAPTER 2

Moving Applications to the Cloud

"For every dollar we spend in this "world of the cloud," we reuse what we already have, and we see a three- to four-dollar greater return. And that is why our evolution into the cloud has become so important to us."

Jim Fowler, Chief Information Officer, General Electric

It Starts with Application Transformation

Cloud transformation is already underway at every organization, often without the knowledge of the IT staff. Cloud and mobility are changing how, where, and when we work. Today, platforms like LinkedIn for professional development, Workday for human resources, ServiceNow for customer support, NetSuite for ERP, and Slack, Yammer, and Skype for collaboration have become the business productivity tools of choice. And, of course, many of your users spend inordinate amounts of time on social media platforms like Twitter, Instagram, and Facebook. Meanwhile, streaming music and video sites drive up bandwidth consumption.

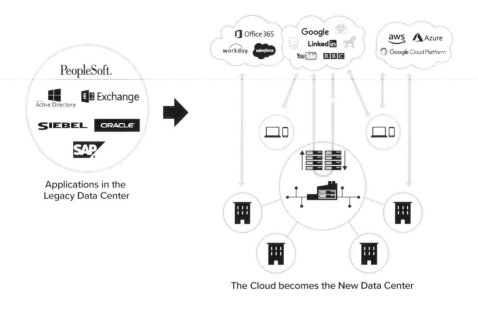

Figure 2.1 Applications are moving from the data center to the cloud

Transitioning to SaaS

The move to the cloud typically comes in stages. The first stage is invariably the use of critical business applications that are hosted in the cloud—software as a service (SaaS), the best example of which is Salesforce. The advantages of SaaS for customers are apparent: minimal capital outlay, no annual maintenance fees, consistent support, easy self-service, and continuous improvement as bugs are fixed and features added with zero friction. Open the application on a Monday morning and there could be dozens of new capabilities added since the previous week, all requiring no testing or upgrade cycles for the customer to schedule.

The most dramatic change impacting organizations today is the rapid move to Office 365, Microsoft's SaaS offering for its office productivity applications. Gone are the days of managing Exchange servers with their SQL backends and high-availability redundancies. Storage with OneDrive and collaboration with SharePoint, all tied to one easy-to-manage Active Directory instance, complete the offering.

Moving Internal Applications to the Public Cloud

SaaS applications are just the first step in a cloud journey. What are organizations doing about internally developed applications? Most organizations maintain hundreds if not thousands of their own applications. This is the next phase of the cloud journey: moving those internal applications to a cloud environment, whether it is on the public cloud such as Amazon Web Services (AWS), Microsoft Azure, or Google Cloud, or in a private cloud in the corporate data center.

Cloud service providers are facilitating this transition by providing more tools and resources to help organizations re-host and re-factor their applications on their infrastructure through platform as a service (PaaS). The rapid adoption of PaaS is growing as reflected in recent reported public cloud revenue growth.[2]

Leveraging Private Cloud

While public cloud adoption is growing at a fast pace, some companies are choosing to put their heavily regulated data in the private cloud due to stringent regulatory or government requirements. These options are becoming widely adopted with various vendors such as VMware offering hosted and on-premises options. AWS GovCloud and Azure Government are some examples of highly regulated and air-gapped cloud environments built to help

---

2   Gartner Forecasts Worldwide Public Cloud Revenue to Grow 21.4 Percent in 2018
https://www.gartner.com/en/newsroom/press-releases/2018-04-12-gartner-forecasts-worldwide-public-cloud-revenue-to-grow-21-percent-in-2018

companies take advantage of the cloud while maintaining all the security and compliance requirements that were previously available on-premises.[3]

Enabling Application Transformation

Whether IT leaders like it or not, the business starts to use these applications and services even before IT can have a say or impose controls. Often the complaint is that IT processes for incorporating new capabilities are too slow. A marketing team can launch a website, contract with a lead funnel management solution like Marketo, and plug into Salesforce without consulting the IT department. This leads to a plethora of data stores, multiple credentialing systems—each a privacy breach waiting to happen—and all without appropriate controls.

The same arguments are heard when employees branch out beyond consuming SaaS applications and start to build applications in the cloud. This so-called shadow IT is often attributed to rogue actors but, in reality, it is natural for a team to want the ease of deployment of spinning up compute resources on AWS or Azure without all of the constraints that the IT department imposes for specifying, purchasing, configuring, and maintaining standalone servers in the data center.

Protecting this access poses additional challenges because now the most critical data and services are being exposed. While a traditional VPN may provide the needed access controls, it is complicated and expensive to maintain and is often one of the top headaches of the IT security team.

---

3 Worldwide Spending on Cloud IT Infrastructure Continued Its Double-Digit Growth Rate in the Second Quarter of 2018, Accounting for Nearly Half of Overall IT Infrastructure Spending, According to IDC https://www.idc.com/getdoc.jsp?containerId=prUS44358318

Larry Biagini, former CIO of GE, declares, that "It is not for IT to say 'no,' but to support the needs of the business." And the users have spoken. They have initiated a move to the cloud that is transformative. The cloud is replacing the data center for application hosting and will eventually replace it for even the most critical transactions.

As we will see in the following chapters, every cloud journey includes the three-part question about what to do with applications as outlined in Figure 2.2: Should I lift and shift, do partial refactoring, or complete refactoring? Some applications may move to a hybrid model, in which the front end is hosted in the cloud while the backend transaction processing and the data remains in the data center. IT has to understand which applications are right to be migrated to the cloud based on the following three approaches:

Lift & Shift	Partial Refactoring	Refactoring
Company Directory, News, Intranet	Content Management System, HRIS	Transaction System, Finances, ERP

Figure 2.2 Approaches for migrating applications to the cloud

Lift and Shift. This approach is for those applications that can be easily moved to the cloud with no modifications. Anything that was already delivered via the web internally can be moved to the cloud. This could include the company directory, HR communications, and help-desk contact forms.

Partial Refactoring. In this case, there may be some minor changes required to move an application to the cloud. Perhaps the backend database has to be standardized or changed. Hardcoded destinations such as IP addresses ideally should be made variable. The same goes for access controls that may be embedded in the application code. Once moved to the cloud, these cannot risk being exposed.

Refactoring. Here, the organization decides to completely rewrite the application. It may call for a new development environment, new coding languages, and new ways to think about applications that can be exposed to partners, customers, and employees, no matter where they are in the world.

Cloud transformation requires a shift in thinking and often implies a change in the makeup of your IT staff. On the one hand, cloud transformation obviates much of the need for networking, system administration, and data center operations. On the other hand, development resources have to be re-trained to think about how applications are developed, delivered, and maintained as highlighted in Figure 2.3.

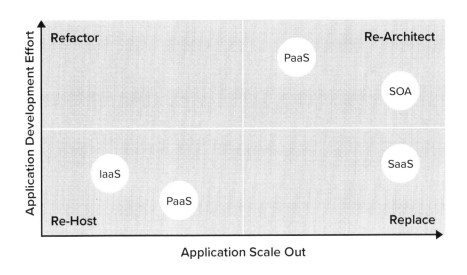

Figure 2.3 Application migration and modernization strategies

Schneider Electric

SaaS as the catalyst for energy management leader's cloud transformation journey

Company:	**Schneider Electric**	Revenue:	**$32 billion**
Sector:	**Listed Company**	Employees:	**144,000**
Driver:	**Hervé Coureil**	Countries:	**100+**
Role:	**Chief Digital Officer**	Locations:	**290**

Company IT Footprint: Schneider Electric is a French multinational corporation that specializes in energy management and automation solutions, spanning hardware, software, and services. Schneider's IT footprint spans over 100,000 connected users in 100 countries.

"Many companies look at "cloud-first" without assessing the network changes this entails. When we started to adopt cloud-delivered applications, we had to understand how our network architecture would be impacted by the cloud. There is a pretty significant network transformation required."

Hervé Coureil, Chief Digital Officer, Schneider Electric

Schneider Electric is one of the largest industrial equipment manufacturers in the world. For them, the move to cloud was precipitated by SaaS as an early customer of Salesforce, and it became a global initiative. Schneider characterizes digital transformation for them as an initiative that goes beyond technology to encompass their customer experience, user experience, and business in general.

Hervé Coureil, Chief Digital Officer of Schneider Electric, describes his organization's cloud transformation journey.

In the words of Hervé Coureil:

At Schneider Electric, our cloud journey began with the move to Salesforce. It became a global initiative that succeeded, and we leveraged that success for everything that came after.

I have been with the company for quite a long time. I started in finance and did a lot of M&A work. When we acquired APC in 2007, I was sent there to drive the merger integration with the title CFO. It was an opportunity to see what happens after the M&A, instead of just orchestrating the deal.

During that time, I realized that information technology was on the critical path to drive business convergence and integration. I also developed a keen interest in security. Schneider at that time had started a program to integrate IT across all of its businesses. The company decided to invest in technology and created the position of global CIO, which fell to me. The CIOs from all of the countries would report to this position. Soon after that, digital transformation became a super-hot topic.

Digital transformation goes well beyond technology to our customer experience, our user experience, and business in general. Last year, we created a digital team that would help us in that digital transformation journey. We took into account sales support, automation, and other projects.

That's why I moved to the role of Chief Digital Officer. It's quite a large team, including a new global CIO who reports directly to me.

The three stages of cloud transformation

The cloud is an enabler from a number of perspectives. It was not completely linear, but there were three distinct stages.

Stage 1: Started with software as a service. Schneider was an early customer of Salesforce. We saw SaaS as a way to enable our transformation. Leveraging SaaS also made a lot of sense for bringing together organizations as a result of many acquisitions. One of the gains was in speed of deployment.

Stage 2: We looked at cloud as a way to transform our infrastructure. Transforming the network is required to take advantage of the cloud.

Stage 3: Involved the cloud and the internet of things to provide new services to our customers. We could not do that without the cloud and mobility—the two mega-trends.

Wide-usage of SaaS applications

We just finalized a major undertaking to move to Office 365 backed by Box for file sharing and storage.

It's difficult to quantify how many sanctioned SaaS applications we have. I would estimate somewhere between 50 and 100. Counting the number of applications is a very common problem. We also took another look at our toolsets for monitoring the applications used in our network. Now we use Zscaler to monitor and notify us of application usage.

Our SaaS applications are segmented into three categories:

1. Internal applications that are connected to single sign-on and managed by us.
2. Applications that we might get alerts on—things like who is using them and how much.
3. Applications that we ban and block.

The migration of internal applications

We used to be a Lotus Notes user. Over the years, we had developed thousands of custom applications for Lotus. One of the big things we are doing in migrating to Office 365 is that we are working on moving as many of those Lotus functions as possible. We had a governance issue at one point, and it was impossible to know how all those applications were being used and what data they were using, and we tried to retire any application that was not needed anymore. We also looked at every application that was developed that could be used in the existing landscape. We had quite a few applications that had been developed on Lotus Notes that would be better served by Salesforce, so we migrated them. In the case of no existing application, we are developing them natively in the cloud. Our partners are instrumental in making that happen.

We do a little bit of both internal and external application development. We are relying on partners but some applications are developed in-house. One of the big challenges is that many of our applications were deployed ten years ago, and the people who developed them are no longer with the organization. Some of the applications had been developed by citizen developers—people who were not even part of the IT organization. There is very limited tribal knowledge remaining for some of the things that were in use. That meant we had to engage in a little digital archeology exercise to reverse engineer the applications and re-develop them for the cloud.

Framework and controls to build right applications for the cloud

We are aware that without careful planning moving to the cloud can pose new challenges. Our goal is to create local environments, so people can develop workflows and simple applications. Rather than slow things down by banning these quick and effective developments, we want to create an environment that is supportive of them.

On the one hand, we want to enable the development of applications, but at the same time, we do not want to create more technical debt. We strive for an empowerment framework. We want everyone to be able to build what they need. So we have two control points:

1. Go through the main portal to determine if we already have a suitable application. It's a very simple process to search and discover apps. The internal customer should make sure the application was not developed somewhere else. In one case, we had a request come through and quickly determined that a team in Italy had already developed something that met the need.

2. Downstream, the second control is an internal privacy and security certification. We want to make sure that we are dotting the i's and crossing the t's when it comes to security. So we vet the applications to ensure they do not introduce a privacy issue, perhaps by collecting data, or open up a security issue.

While it is not written in stone, we have a high-level philosophy of all new applications being built for the cloud.

Our network transformation: MPLS to direct connection to cloud

Many companies look at "cloud-first" without assessing the network changes this entails. When we started to adopt cloud-delivered applications, we had to understand how our network architecture would be impacted by the cloud. There is a pretty significant network transformation required. First, we looked at the architecture: MPLS and the number of network access points versus direct connections to cloud providers.

"When we started to adopt cloud-delivered applications, we had to understand how our network architecture would be impacted by the cloud."

The second thing that's relevant from a network standpoint is the security of local internet breakouts from each office. That is where we invested in Zscaler.

We have more local breakouts than we used to have. Before the cloud, internet access was a second-class citizen. After the cloud, it becomes a critical element of our network usage.

We used to have firewalls and numerous other hardware appliances, but now we have a cloud-first strategy that Zscaler has allowed us to do.

While local breakouts provide one benefit—cost savings—another has been quality of service. Schneider is a global company with over 100,000 connected users. Many countries don't necessarily have the best local network architecture, and one of the things we were trying achieve was a good response time globally.

On top of that, we have a mobile strategy. We try to give people voice access to the network, and we enable BYOD (bring your own device) in every country where possible.

Classifying and protecting critical data

Our security strategy focuses on protecting the crown jewels, the most significant intellectual property in the company. This approach means that we have to be good at data classification. When identifying those crown jewels to protect, the natural tendency is to be super conservative; everything is a crown jewel. To instill discipline in the process, we designated one person whose role is to look at the identification of those crown jewels: our confidential information, sensitive IP, and of course, privacy data. We try to keep the crown jewel category very limited.

When we certify each internal application, we look at both security and privacy criteria. We have a Data Protection Officer running our EU General Data Protection Regulation (GDPR) program. When we certify a new application, we do a privacy assessment at the same time as security to ensure that we are only collecting the data we need, that we properly notify the end users when we collect it, and we take precautions to protect it.

"Our security strategy focuses on protecting the crown jewels."

Security: the key to cloud transformation

Security is an obvious priority. Without it, the rest of cloud transformation cannot happen. We have been thinking a lot about the security model and considering how to look at the cloud security we wanted to adapt.

Security is never over. Incident response is a big topic, as is network segmentation, network monitoring, and endpoint protection. We have eight or nine security initiatives currently.

While data loss prevention (DLP) is one of the things we looked at, we decided it is a very heavy burden to take on. There are so many ways to exfiltrate data. So, to begin, we have taken a very light approach. Applications should be DLP-secure at the application level. Since we are inspecting traffic in both directions, it is a simple matter of looking for common things like personally identifiable information (PII) and set an alert or block them.

We're using sandboxing technology to stay on top of advanced malware. We have deployed the Zscaler sandbox in the cloud to identify malware in files and internet sites our users may visit. We also believe that having a centralized identity management system is important to a successful cloud strategy. We use Active Directory and another product for single sign-on.

It is not very original, but you can feel very safe inside of a castle—but you don't see the known unknowns on your extended perimeter. Our cloud strategy allows us to have a much more global approach.

Legacy approaches to security are complicated, requiring isolated mini-castles in every office. You have to replicate your headquarters security stack in every location. The cloud allows us to be much better at managing multiple sites in multiple countries with one control plane.

Challenges along the way

There was a bit of resistance to our cloud transformation, but it wasn't massive. For us, the defining point was the global move to Salesforce, which was a great success. We managed to embrace it relatively quickly. From there, we had created our first success story. We had deployed it faster than we would have deployed a traditional on-premises solution.

We had a couple of issues in our journey to the cloud. The main problem we had was quality of service in certain places. The experience in the United States with Salesforce was not replicated everywhere, and we learned the hard way that some countries do not have the best infrastructure. We had to rethink the network globally.

While measuring results is important, we are not looking at one golden metric that will summarize all the good things we achieved through cloud transformation. But every time we launch a project, we do monitor its success. When we deployed the custom application environment, we looked at how we are modernizing the application base. For every application we are decommissioning, we have a gain we can chalk up. Cloud is now so pervasive in everything we do that we look at the metrics of utilization.

How is internet usage growing? Since our initial move to Salesforce, we have seen cloud usage grow steadily. That first step started us on this journey.

What not to do:

- I would advise against going too broad. Don't try to boil the ocean and do everything at one time. Deploy a pilot, have a success story, and build on that.

- Do not ignore the network implications. Look at the network architecture at the beginning of the cloud adoption. Try to get ahead of the problems.

What to do:

- Cloud is a means to an end. You want to create customer and business value. Cloud enables machine learning, which enables voice. Voice has its own benefits that lead to collaboration opportunities.

- Cloud allows you to connect sites together more quickly. Just point all the users at the apps.

- When talking to my peers in the industry, a lot of the conversations I have revolved around big questions. What's next? What is the next wave? How do we prepare for the new trends? We are forward-looking, while keeping security concerns front and center.

FrieslandCampina

*An International Dairy Conglomerate's Network
and Security Transformation Journey*

Company:	**FrieslandCampina**	Revenue:	**$14 billion**
Sector:	**Dairy**	Employees:	**20,000**
Driver:	**Erik Klein**	Countries:	**34**
Role:	**Infrastructure Architect**	Locations:	**120**

Company IT Footprint: FrieslandCampina has 120 locations. They employ over 20,000 people worldwide, but, because those people work in shifts, the number of endpoints are not related to the number of employees. Within the office and industrial workspace, there are about 7,000 to 8,000 endpoints. They currently also have over 80 factories worldwide.

"I'm looking towards making the network totally irrelevant in the next five to seven years. The network will only be a transport mechanism that makes sure the application goes from A to B, but the data security itself is completely embedded in the communication stream."

Erik Klein, Infrastructure Architect, FrieslandCampina

FrieslandCampina is a global producer of milk products and has created a sophisticated network to provide consistent and secure global connectivity. Erik Klein, lead infrastructure architect, tells their network and security transformation story.

In the words of Erik Klein:

Bringing milk products to the world

I joined FrieslandCampina in 2012. We are a global producer of milk products—we make cheese, infant and toddler nutrition, yogurts, skimmed and semi-skimmed milk, condensed milk, and health foods for athletes. We are based in the Netherlands, and over time we have expanded into other countries, such as Indonesia, Vietnam, Nigeria, Ghana, the U.S., and many others.

IT has an important role in manufacturing goods. From a production perspective, the availability of the operations technology (OT) environment (which is IT within the production environment with specific requirements) has a huge impact. For example, the raw milk can't be stored for more than seventy-two hours. Any longer and it gets discarded, but it can't be thrown away into a sewer, so it is a costly process to dispose of the spoiled product. Therefore, OT is used within the production environment to make sure that the production processes aren't disrupted and work within the strict timeframes.

Within the OT environment, with the introduction of next generation PLCs (programmable logic controls), smart sensors, and other IoT developments, the number of IP-based endpoints will grow considerably over time.

Currently, we have about 80 factories worldwide. Some are more traditional, but some are really sophisticated and the Smart Factory is emerging. Therefore, the number of endpoints will grow in the OT environment.

Our cloud transformation

By the end of 2013, the cloud hype cycle started and there were more and more people looking at software as a service, localized content, and moving stuff to the cloud—in our case, Amazon Web Services.

"We needed to go into a transformation from a private MPLS-centered network to a public internet-centric network."

Eventually, we realized, when going in that direction, the wide area network we had was no longer valid. We needed to go into a transformation from a private MPLS-centered network to a public internet-centric network.

At that time, the designs we made consisted of several boxes on location, and we realized that this would be too complicated and expensive to execute. So in 2014, we embarked on the transformation journey by moving the centralized proxy server to the cloud with the Zscaler cloud service, but still relying on the capabilities of Cisco routers for all other functions.

As cybersecurity became more of an issue, the Zscaler Cloud Firewall came into play. Moving security to the cloud was harder, because I had some internal push back, and there were some reorganization issues. But in 2016, we started a project to extend the boundaries of our network from a stateful firewall on a Cisco router at the FrieslandCampina location to cloud security, the Zscaler Cloud Firewall.

From every location, we then built IPsec tunnels to the Zscaler security service and used the proxy functionality as well as firewall functionality of Zscaler.

To overcome the limitations using PAC (proxy auto-configuration) files in the browser to get to the internet, we also transferred the routing within the whole LAN environment, so that the default route from every location would end up at the security layer of Zscaler. And that's where we are today.

And then it was time for testing dynamic application routing.

Why secure internet local breakouts?

There are two reasons why we switched from a centralized proxy environment to the cloud-based proxy environment with local breakouts. Firstly, from a marketing perspective, the driver to break out locally was to get localized content. The web servers that you're connecting to from each country should automatically give the content of the website in the local language, for example.

Secondly, FrieslandCampina had been using a number of different SaaS applications worldwide, so having it all centrally break out was, from a performance perspective, not a way forward. Also, the web content became richer and files were getting bigger, so there was more data to transport. From a localized content perspective, and the fact that users are using more and more SaaS applications, we realized that we would need to bring the end user to the internet (cloud) quicker.

Except for our private cloud, direct-connected VPC (virtual private cloud) on AWS—and we have connected that to our MPLS backbone so that's still going over an MPLS link—everything else is being offloaded at the local site level and then travels to the closest Zscaler data center based on lowest latency, with a second closest Zscaler data center as backup. We do a measurement every six months to see if indeed those Zscaler nodes are still the quickest to reach.

Moving applications to AWS

FrieslandCampina is currently migrating applications to AWS based on various criteria, such as those applications that only need to be accessed at certain times. This service can't be provided by our existing hosting provider, and keeping those servers at their location will be too expensive. On the other hand, T-Systems couldn't always meet the requirements of the applications, resulting in an instance that was too big (too expensive) or too small (poor performance). And thirdly, AWS gives us the flexibility to temporarily upscale and downscale when required. With the capabilities of AWS, we could tailor to the actual requirements of the applications.

Last but not least, since not all applications are 24/7, we could use AWS elasticity to turn them off on the weekends, saving money in the process.

"The 2016 phase of the network transformation went very quickly and was completely non-disruptive."

Improving SaaS access

In the early days, when we moved to the cloud proxy, we had our share of difficulties with the performance of Office 365. We really struggled to get that done correctly and have good performance now.

The 2016 phase of the network transformation went very quickly and was completely non-disruptive—people didn't even know we moved security to Zscaler. Nobody really noticed that we went from centralized to decentralized, except that some of the applications became quicker.

Also, Zscaler was very quick in communicating what they were doing about cyber security threats like, but not limited to, WannaCry and NotPetya. They were quicker to communicate the impact within their environment than other partners. They really did a good job on that one.

Deploying SD-WAN

Right now, we are going towards a full SD-WAN (software-defined wide area network). Our strategy involves connecting five FrieslandCampina locations to the SD-WAN environment, and that the SD-WAN environment has an NNI (network-to-network interface) with our existing Verizon network. With a full-blown SD-WAN deployment our redundancy plan includes redundant internet lines and universal customer premises equipment.

For locations that use applications that require MPLS services, a fit for purpose MPLS line that is smaller than our legacy MPLS circuit is supplied. Historically for every location, except locations with call center functionality, the MPLS line was approximately 5 megabits per second, while the internet lines are a lot bigger. We also have a failover from MPLS to the internet and the two internet lines back each other up. Our goal is to guarantee an experience level agreement (XLA) at the application level, rather than a service level agreement (SLA) based on availability and time to repair. We are aiming for predictable behavior and end-user experience on an application-based context (device, location, connectivity).

The SD-WAN has what they call universal CPEs at each location. And those universal CPEs will have network function virtualization on them. Actually it's a device for compute and storage with a hypervisor, which runs virtual services which are required by either the SD-WAN service itself or the application acceleration. Other virtual network functions can be added if and when required. There will be a growing number of network function virtualizations that we can deploy on those devices.

Picking an SD-WAN partner

In 2017, we initiated an RFI for, amongst other services, a new WAN service.

The vendors invited to the RFI were only given business requirements and we asked them to really innovate with a disruptive approach. We selected eight vendors to enter the RFP phase, and we started eliminating vendors based on their offering and presentation of the solution. In the end, three vendors were selected to give us their best and final offer, namely NTT, Interoute (both proposing the Silver Peak SD-WAN solution), and Verizon (proposing a combination of Viptela and Riverbed).

As part of the RFP process, we asked each vendor to present a reference customer where they had already deployed the proposed solution. And based on discussions with those customers, we made the final selection. The vendor testimonials were very important to us in the final phase of the RFP process.

Things to consider

- Do not invest in a traditional network. Don't do any investments in your existing MPLS with an internet backup network. That's old school. Just make sure that you know how your traffic is routing—so where your end users are and where your applications are—and make sure that you create a network where, based on the applications, the quickest, most efficient route will be taken. In the end, users are not interested in technology, they are only concerned that the applications they are working with on a day-to-day basis perform well and perform constantly. If you have an application that has a 2.5 millisecond response time throughout all of Asia, nobody is complaining. But if you have one country that has a response time of one and another of four, then they start talking to each other and start complaining.

- People are traveling more and working outside of the office, and those people are diverse. Currently, we are bringing people that are roaming back into our network via two central remote access (VPN concentrated) locations. With the use of tools like the Zscaler App, we are looking at alternatives to connect roaming users to internal applications.

- In the end, if you have your software-defined wide area network, local area network, and software-defined data centers, you need an orchestrator of orchestrators above that to make sure the policies you set on an application, or at a higher level, flows down to the LAN, the WAN, and the data center. And the next step is to invest in security in the session between consumer and application.

- I'm looking towards making the network totally irrelevant in the next five to seven years. The network will only be a transport mechanism that makes sure the application goes from A to B, but the data security itself is completely embedded in the communication stream. For example, based on the identity of the client and on the identity of the application, a secure communication will be set up between them. That will be my next focus, and will be around the 2025-28 timeframe. It could happen sooner, but developments within our company need a business case for change; there needs to be funding for it, and so on.

Not only is the development of the technology driving this, but also the adaptation and the willingness to spend money in new areas.

Chapter 2 Takeaways

The cloud is the new corporate data center. As applications migrate to cloud infrastructure, this invariably creates opportunities and challenges for CIOs, CTOs, and CISOs. To ensure a successful migration, it's vital that the business objectives are clearly defined, stakeholders identified, and strategy and priorities established and widely communicated.

Key considerations for embarking on your application transformation journey:

- List and prioritize your applications

- Consider data security and risks on an application basis—evaluate and classify each application, rank the cost and impact to the organization, determine mission criticality, productivity impact

- List top business and technical goals for each application—compliance requirements, user experience, reliability, performance, licensing costs

- Analyze each application to determine which can be migrated quickly to the cloud and which would require more transformation effort—architectures, where it is hosted; are they shared services; platforms and programming languages used

- Engage, inform, and train key stakeholders in the process

In the next chapter, we'll discuss how application transformation drives network transformation, and how this next stage is pivotal in enabling digital transformation for the enterprise.

CHAPTER 3

From Hub-and-Spoke to Hybrid Networks

"When faced with having to deploy and manage little stacks of iron in over 360 locations, my immediate thought was going to a cloud-based solution."

Ken Athanasiou, Chief Information Security Officer, AutoNation

---

Application transformation drives network transformation

As applications move to the cloud and the cloud becomes the new center of gravity, the internet becomes the new corporate network. When this happens, backhauling traffic to the data center no longer makes sense. Traffic should, and eventually will, find a way to take the path of least resistance and go direct-to-cloud, providing a fast and seamless user experience. Backhauling traffic destined for the internet to the enterprise data center is inefficient and expensive. Additionally, requiring remote users to be on the corporate network detracts from their productivity and exposes that network to abusers. The driving principle is to quickly connect any user on any device to any application wherever they are in the world. All this while protecting the data and the end-user device at all times.

Hub-and-spoke network architecture has served IT for 25+ years

Corporate wide area networks (WANs) were originally deployed to interconnect the local area networks (LANs) in each office and data center. There were many protocols in use on these LANs, from Token Ring to Ethernet or even AppleTalk. As the corporate world moved to Windows for desktops and NT for servers, the standard for corporate networking became the internet TCP/IP protocol stack.

WANs too began to change. They had to interoperate with TCP/IP networks, and MPLS became a way to accomplish this while preserving some of the services and features of other protocols. Over time, these MPLS circuits became almost 100 percent TCP/IP traffic, but the dedicated circuits sold by carriers preserved the reliability and service guarantees that customers demanded—and paid for. The rise of networking vendors like Cisco was linked to the widespread adoption of today's WAN and TCP/IP protocols.

As critical business resources like Salesforce and Office 365 move to the cloud, the underlying weaknesses in network architectures are discovered. When the data center was once the center of the universe it was logical to make investments in wide area network infrastructure to connect the remote office to the data center. This is commonly referred to as a hub-and-spoke architecture.

Traffic moves from remote offices to the nearest hub, a central or regional data center.

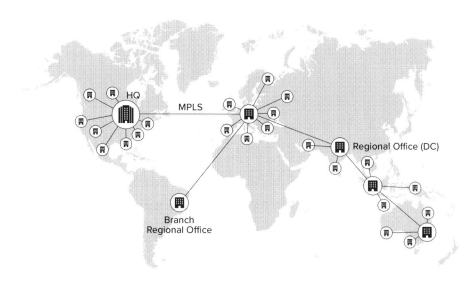

Figure 3.1 A hub-and-spoke network model connects remote offices to data centers

These are the three challenges cloud adoption has created for traditional hub-and-spoke architectures:

1. Backhauling traffic ultimately destined for the internet creates a bad user experience. Poor response times of SaaS applications and general internet sites cause users to complain. They get a better experience from home than they do on the corporate network.

2. As more and more traffic is destined for the internet, backhauling costs are skyrocketing. Some applications like Office 365 are bandwidth intensive, and the organization pays to transport that traffic both to and from the hub.

3. It becomes increasingly complex to architect the traffic flows to maintain usability with routers, switches, and management tools deployed to ensure a consistent experience.

One parallel to this analogy is airline travel. Frequent travelers are familiar with a hub-and-spoke design. Many airlines force you through three or four hubs. Instead of taking the direct route from one city to another you take long detours to one of those hubs where you encounter delays, lost luggage, and lost time; a poor user experience. The hubs—major airports—are upgraded continuously, and passengers are forced through more and more complicated routes as they make their way between gates. At Charles De Gaulle airport, the hub outside Paris that is arguably one of best examples of such complication, you may find yourself on a short layover rushing to your gate, only to be dumped back into the arrival hall and have to go through security again to catch your next flight. Similar traffic disruptions and complications occur in your hub-and-spoke network architecture.

"Imagine flying from New York to Chicago via Dallas or Houston."
Jay Chaudhry, CEO and Chairman, Zscaler

Hybrid networking is a logical and low-risk first step

As more and more traffic is destined for the internet, the only way to accommodate this traffic is to move to a hybrid network. For each branch of a regional office in a hybrid network:

- Internet-bound traffic is routed to the internet or the cloud over a local internet connection which is often broadband; and

- Corporate traffic is routed to the data center over the traditional MPLS network.

This helps to save on MPLS bandwidth costs and ensures an optimal user experience.

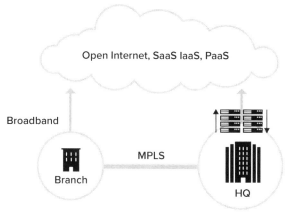

Figure 3.2 A hybrid network

Incremental path for local internet breakouts

Over time, there is a path to transition from a hybrid network to that envisioned by many of the enterprise IT leaders in this book: direct-to-internet and cloud connectivity for all traffic.

Figure 3.3 Direct-to-cloud and internet connectivity

Of course, there is resistance to making too abrupt a move. The idea is appealing because MPLS circuit costs are staggering, but what about reliability? Can internet connections be counted on to deliver an always-up connection that MPLS circuits are known to provide? More and more vendors are now offering SLAs for reliability, and bandwidth quality of service over the internet.

In most regions, broadband connections are so inexpensive that two or more can be purchased at a fraction of the cost of MPLS circuits; anywhere from one half to one-tenth the cost.

Hub-and-spoke networking over MPLS gives way to local internet breakouts. Cost savings, enhanced user experience, and simplification are the result.

Network transformation does not have to be disruptive. It is nothing like the disruption caused by selecting a new ERP vendor with the cost and delays these projects incur. You can take incremental steps, first moving to a hybrid network then cutting the cord and going internet-only in select locations. It can be a measured transformation.

For example, the concept of a local internet breakout is not new. Many companies are already deploying internet-only branch offices. GE [Chapter 1] and AutoNation [Chapter 4] realized the value of the internet-only branch and embraced it years ago.

SD-WAN simplifies local internet breakouts

Software-defined wide area networks (SD-WANs) can make local internet breakouts easier to manage. They can be easily deployed at hundreds of branch offices. Managed from the cloud, these lightweight appliances use software policies to determine whether traffic should be routed to the internet over local connections—including broadband and cellular networks—or routed back to the corporate data center over private circuits. The days of logging into a remote appliance and issuing command line instructions are coming to an end.

In a world that requires multiple networks for optimal connectivity, it is critical to have a flexible software-based branch network. The branch network must make decisions on which network to use based on the applications and performance requirements rather than by IP addresses and routes. SD-WAN devices excel at integrating switching, routing, and path selection functionality. While they can offer basic security, most enterprises direct traffic from each branch office to a cloud security provider to secure their SD-WAN.

Siemens

Global Network and Security Transformation

Company:	**Siemens**	Revenue:	**$108 billion**
Sector:	**Conglomerate**	Employees:	**360,000**
Driver:	**Frederik Janssen**	Countries:	**192**
Role:	**Global Head of Infrastructure**	Locations:	**2,200**

Company IT Footprint: Siemens' IT infrastructure covers 192 countries globally. They serve 360,000 end users—employees—and another approximately 70,000 external contractors. Their server and application landscape encompasses 10,000 applications and around 60,000 servers. In addition to the 450,000 clients and internal/external employees, they manage approximately 200,000 mobile devices.

"The internet will become the new corporate network."

Frederik Janssen, Global Head of Infrastructure, Siemens

Siemens is one of the largest manufacturers in the world. The company saw a proliferation of mobile endpoints in their environment in addition to having to secure and support their highly distributed and mobile workforce. With over 64% of their traffic per site going to the internet, they had reached a tipping point whereby the internet was becoming their new corporate network.

Frederik Janssen, the global head of infrastructure, shares how he led the charge to improve IT systems through cloud transformation for his organization.

The Siemens transformation story

I have been working in IT for almost 17 years, ten of those at Siemens. I studied computer science and have held various roles at the company. In the beginning, I was mainly focused on software development, software engineering, software architecture, database systems, database development, and web applications.

The squeaky wheel gets the job

One day, seven years ago, I was in a meeting with our CIO in which we were discussing how our infrastructure was running. He offered me the challenge to take on the responsibility for our infrastructure, and I agreed.

> "We knew early on that the cloud was going to revolutionize the way we consumed IT services."

And that's when my infrastructure career started. I was always keen on identifying options and investigating how we could really optimize our infrastructure by minimizing manual tasks and thereby eliminating typical errors and failures. Five years ago, our journey included many projects with a lot of different technological topics: we had rollouts of new operating systems, introduced big technological changes, and introduced cloud computing into our manager desks at Siemens.

We knew early on that the cloud was going to revolutionize the way we consumed IT services, and how we developed applications.

Today I have global responsibility for our Center of Expertise for Infrastructure, and I lead a service portfolio along with lifecycle management. That also includes strategy, innovation, and development of new services, including the transition to new services. My team is responsible from cradle to grave—we have responsibility for everything we develop with partners and providers throughout the lifetime of the respective services.

Siemens' global IT scope

From a sizing perspective, the Siemens' infrastructure covers 192 countries globally. We serve 360,000 end users—employees—and another approximately 70,000 external contractors. Our server and application landscape encompasses 10,000 applications and around 60,000 servers. We are also heavy users of Microsoft servers and Microsoft Windows operating systems.

It wasn't just cloud computing that was on the horizon for the company, but also consumerization trends. We have seen an explosion of mobile endpoints in our environment. In addition to the 450,000 clients and internal/external employees, we managed 50% of all devices used. That made it about 200,000 devices from a mobile perspective.

We have already been able to significantly consolidate the number of applications we run, so we are now down to around 7,000 corporate applications, and around 500 applications that I would call corporate mission-critical applications.

Storage has been growing 25% annually

Five years ago, we had around three to four petabytes of storage for end users and roughly the same amount for databases. Since then, we have seen a significant increase. We now have growth rates up around 25% annually. That is challenging us to also identify ways to modernize our storage environment. We heavily leverage our network to push data to the cloud and to make sure that we can decommission old storage components and hardware.

The need for an infrastructure overhaul

We realized we needed to evolve our infrastructure to be more efficient—to help us embrace new technological possibilities, minimize costs, and provide us with more flexibility

We also needed to ensure that our users, managers, IT departments, and application owners had infrastructure in place that would allow them to run their applications at scale and drive greater productivity

We addressed this infrastructure transformation with a few different approaches, with top management aggressively championing the initiative. You will not get very far if you don't have a full management buy-in to really transform the environment. As the complexity of infrastructure is typically very much underestimated, especially when it comes to things like network or identity and access management or server architectures, you have to "slice the elephant." And that's what we tried to do.

Data location poses a compliance problem

First, we tried to manage the overall image of the cloud. As a German multinational company with cloud computing, it was complicated to drive the transition from the U.S. There were several security concerns on our side, especially when you talk to people from the information security or privacy protection departments. They had their concerns, especially with the Patriot Act and other U.S. government-related actions, potentially leading to certain security or data leakage issues that we were committed to preventing. We also had to have discussions about competitiveness and intellectual property protection—business concerns.

It was time to migrate applications

After we addressed the fundamental changes for moving data, moving applications, and moving infrastructure into the cloud, we had to execute a holistic plan to "slice the elephant." So, by gaining trust and providing fast results we added benefits to the business. We raised the confidence at Siemens and became more supportive when it came to cloud transformation activities.

Rehost on infrastructure as a service (IaaS)
Refactor for platform as a service (PaaS)
Revise for IaaS or PaaS
Rebuild on PaaS
Replace with software as a service (SaaS)

Figure 3.4 The Gartner Five Rs—Five Ways to Migrate Applications to the Cloud

First, we tried to figure out what could be replaced by a new model, in terms of moving it into a SaaS environment and therefore consuming it out of the cloud. We introduced ServiceNow, Salesforce, and Office 365, which we had previously introduced into the company.

Next, we implemented additional validation or evaluation of the applications and decided whether we could just re-host them in terms of moving the application or put them as-is into the cloud environment.

Transforming the network to provide the right connectivity

We realized early on that our traffic pattern, overall, was changing significantly. We had reached a point where 64% of traffic on average, per site, was going to the internet. So, the traffic pattern in itself was very much becoming internet-centric.

We tried to clearly evangelize the story internally by saying that the internet will be the next corporate network. We stressed that over time, keeping that transition in mind, we are going to have more applications in the cloud than we are running in internal data centers or private cloud data centers, which are still connected to our intranet. We are reaching the tipping point now. Most applications in Siemens will be public cloud based, and therefore, totally connected through the internet.

From a capacity management point of view, we are gradually ramping up internet connectivity in parallel or to coexist with our remaining MPLS private networks. We are currently mobilizing a team that is getting our network to the next level of sophistication, which provides us much more flexibility. Ultimately, we will be introducing internet-only connectivity for around 90% of all sites that we are currently supporting. Siemens maintains around 2,200 sites globally in 192 countries.

With our global WAN carriers, we are required to closely manage interaction, so that we know what steps to execute on from a management point of view. We were quite lucky that we had already been consolidating our carrier infrastructure down to two carriers: one for Germany, and one for the rest of the world. That helped us directly steer activity and was one of the key success factors for our wide area network.

Improving application security

The access to applications was extremely important, especially when we could no longer rely on a secure network. We started off with a clear, strategic direction to all application owners that requested that they consider their application in a way that it would already be exposed to the internet today. In other words, protect yourself without relying on the network.

We introduced single mechanisms that required the user, depending on the confidentiality, to classify an application through multi-factor authentication. We also applied traditional firewall approaches to reduce the number of possible ways to reach the server.

"It is quite a tough challenge to secure a network which you don't control."

As we were moving applications to the cloud and embracing SaaS offerings, we realized that it is quite a tough challenge to secure a network which you don't control. We also maintained outbound and inbound traffic at the same time. Therefore we recognized that our perimeter of policy enforcement and network control is going to be changing. It will not only be in our hands. That was also the point in time when we had been looking at solutions in the market to help us to secure connectivity in the cloud.

Introducing cloud-optimized internet access

During this process, we also found that we had to update our service areas. Thus, we came up with COIA, which stands for cloud-optimized internet access, a term we currently use to communicate internally. In the beginning it was quite a transition, but now every user is aware of the term.

Next, we had to create a security aspect. We decided to introduce Zscaler.

We started with a proxy server based on connectivity to the internet with our outsourcing partner and explored ways to optimize it. One of the first steps was to leverage local internet breakouts. We were riding on the lines of our carriers, and we let Zscaler find the most ideal routes to the next big net-based internet gateway.

Finding the right security partner

Eventually, we found ourselves discussing this with several different carriers and screening the market. For a company the size of Siemens, there were only five or six solutions that we could seriously consider. There was also one very new challenger. Our main carrier approached us and was concerned that we hadn't heard of Zscaler. They brought Zscaler to our attention and explained how Zscaler had quite an interesting solution. They were completely running in the cloud—we would not have to deploy anything in our environment—and they could scale up very, very quickly.

Through their cloud security platform with comprehensive functionality, they offered several things that other providers didn't have.

We knew this was a crucial element in our transition and if we could find a partner who could keep up with the pace we require them to take, then we would be more than happy to embark on that partnership. I think that was the first time we met people from Zscaler, and they were quite different from anyone we had seen before. They approached it completely different- ly; they were cloud native.

We shared with our carrier and with Zscaler what we wanted to do and what our targets were, and it turned out our strategy was completely in line with what Zscaler was envisioning. We were able to execute against this joint vision and rolled out the service in less than twelve months. Since then, we have been able to set a certain track record for introducing cloud-based solutions and optimizing our network architecture.

Building a cloud-first team

We learned that we needed to have a team in place that was fully commit- ted to using the cloud. My advice to other companies would be to careful- ly select their internal team and have an eye on those working from the carrier side.

Planning and understanding your application landscape, along with user requirements, is also a crucial factor.

Troubleshooting is much easier now that we don't have to look at thousands of appliances on the ground. The cloud was a positive change in terms of resiliency and flexibility. It resulted in a very smooth rollout.

Taking on regional issues

You also have to take into consideration embargoed countries or countries with special political or economic circumstances. Just to name a few: Russia, India, China, Iran. These are countries where you, of course, must look a little bit more into the details of how you can drive the change. What can go to the cloud? Where do you have to store it? How do you have to store it? Do you have to have a copy, still, in the country locally? Are there any other legal considerations in each country that you have to respect and follow?

There is plenty to learn, especially when it comes to global deployment. The network is just taking care of the transportation and not the storing of data, especially when it comes to the re-hosting of applications and the storage of data. This is where it can start to become quite a headache.

Improving end-user satisfaction

Our end users are happy with the cloud-optimized internet access as one service, but they are also happy to use evergreen applications, which are updated or enhanced with new features on a monthly or quarterly basis. We do not have the discussions around why is Siemens not using the latest version. I think after some initial growing pains, people are now embracing the change. People are more relaxed about storing data in the cloud.

The first 12 months required some adjustment, but we are now in the phase where people can't imagine going back to the old world, into the old situation.

Cloud transformation has empowered the organization

We have been giving more power to our different divisions and business units, which is providing a certain level of required separation between the groups.

"The higher performance and greater flexibility is helping our end users, in addition to company management and overarching targets."

This separation requires individual customizing, which we love in the cloud—typically creating, then spinning off an old tenant. Multi-tenancy is a standard in the cloud and we require our vendors and application service providers to support it. Therefore, we have a much better chance to react to organizational changes, and we can cater to them from an IT perspective.

For Siemens overall, the cloud is helping us on these macro changes. And for the end users, obviously, we are much faster in terms of our ability to adjust infrastructure, apply new policies, control how people are consuming bandwidth, make sure that business-critical applications get the right priority—and we are able to increase the underlying infrastructure to cover any additional load during peaks.

The higher performance and greater flexibility is helping our end users, in addition to company management and overarching targets.

Gaining new freedom and flexibility

The cloud gave us the ultimate freedom to explore small, new ideas that didn't require a heavy investment in new hardware or infrastructure. And we could do all of it without incurring any commercial risks. The cloud enables us to be more agile by inventing prototypes and including customers in the early stages of development. Our application landscape can now be optimized by using the agility of the cloud in terms of consumption level. We love being more flexible, faster, and able to address business needs as we are going into more prototyping—rapid prototyping—and faster development cycles.

Moving security to the cloud

Everything started when we knew we wanted to optimize how we accessed the internet. We needed a solution that would give us the additional security and protection in the cloud that we were accustomed to on premises. Zscaler Internet Access established distributed policy enforcement points through which all our traffic and regional hubs flowed. We could also use a standard enforcement point to establish and dispatch connectivity for inbound access, which would work with remote connections.

Providing secure access to internal apps

There are certain critical applications that Siemens is not currently considering moving to the cloud due to high sensitivity, such as those that involve financial or internal data. Our next step was to add another level, so that we could run different applications, services, and macro connections through Zscaler Private Access.

We are still in the process of integrating the inbound access with all Siemens' specific tools or applications and services. Identity and access management was one. Here again, the cloud is helping us to just drive standardization to a certain extent so that we are using market-standard authentication.

In the end, the implementation and integration were straightforward. On the one hand, Zscaler is building their solution based on market standards. On the other, our strategy clearly pivots around on market standards which give us the ability to choose platforms and carriers.

Advice to others embarking on a cloud journey

I would advise other companies to create a bold vision and mission statement and to communicate it internally in a very aggressive way. You need to know exactly what you need to make your cloud journey happen and you need to get everyone fully behind it. And then you would also need to support the first movers. You should pick some lighthouse candidates for transformation.

I want to emphasize how important it is to ensure the close interaction and cooperation with respective departments, especially those that are responsible for cyber security or information security, protection, export control, and all the other critical support functions that have a say in the whole process.

You also need to have some users who are actively supporting the journey and who are bringing in some clear perspective that their life has improved since they began using cloud solutions. And of course, you must have a convincing time-scale calculation ready. That means giving it the right level of priority as you eliminate the high costs while you are handing over responsibility to third parties.

You need to focus on your partners and on retaining and building the partnership. This is why Siemens is calling one of the changing pillars of our overall global IT strategy "collaborative IT." It's no longer only up to us as an IT department to run our IT landscape. It's much more about collaborating with our partners to innovate, to go at a certain pace. We are relying on them, on the one hand, to keep up, and on the other hand, to co-innovate the future service offerings, sharpening them for the future.

Things to avoid

What I would really try to avoid is losing focus. If you lose focus and if you're not able to train your staff on the platforms you selected, you might get lost in complexity. And if you have some very complex and hard-to-lift applications, they shouldn't be among the first lighthouse projects.

Careful selection of cloud projects is important, because if you screw up one of the products, it will create a certain noise level that becomes counterproductive. You need to avoid too many negative sentiments from within the organization, which tends to sow doubt about moving data and shifting responsibility into the cloud. These are our main pillars of getting the engine running.

Moving forward

In the future, an important aspect will be managing the landscape of partners, our idea of "collaborative IT." We also want to develop integration based on market standards between the different cloud solutions. Application services will be a vital component of every corporate IT' organization's task. I would also envision that overall, corporate IT departments would reduce their footprint when it comes to internal staff and spend more time managing office IT-related applications and services, because their cloud consumption is going to be the clearly defined new standard.

"The cloud will be our main data center going forward."

At the same time, I do believe that these changes are also fostering collaboration with business units on digitalization. By moving workloads to the cloud, we are freeing up capacity that we can use to work together with the business units on even more sophisticated IT solutions, which will help our BUs to be more efficient and, in the end, more successful in the company.

The cloud will be our main data center going forward. There are some golden nuggets or crown jewels which we would typically not move into the cloud, such as our trust center where we use certificates to identify servers, clients, users, everything. But the number of workloads that still require an old data center presence is very low.

Chapter 3 Takeaways

It is clear that in a cloud and mobile-first world, users should be able to take the most direct path to the applications they need for a business to operate at its best. This necessitates that corporations adopt a "direct-to-cloud" and hybrid network architecture rather than a hub-and-spoke MPLS based architecture. As Siemens exemplifies in this chapter, in the new world the cloud is the new data center and the internet the new corporate network.

As the center of gravity of enterprise IT shifts from the data center to the cloud, where mission-critical applications now reside, so must security architectures change. The old world of applications hosted in the data center has given way to a world of applications in public clouds, private clouds, and SaaS.

The hub-and-spoke models that were so prevalent over the last three decades have to give way to the most direct path to these applications, wherever they re-side. Local breakouts—connecting remote locations directly to the internet—is a preparatory phase to the future when every device will connect directly to the internet.

Key considerations:

- Treat remote offices like remote workers. Connect them directly to the internet. Users will do this no matter what you do especially when things like LTE and 5G are embedded in their devices natively.

- Security based on building a perimeter with firewalls and other traditional security appliances will not be effective. Rather, think about how to se-curely connect a user to the right application or service.

- The network must be transformed. A direct-to-cloud architecture will save money while improving user experience. MPLS will play a reduced role and may be relegated to a position that mainframes have today: legacy.

As the corporate network evolves to direct-to-cloud, legacy castle-and-moat security models built to protect those hubs must also give way to a new architecture—network transformation cannot happen without security transformation. In the next chapter, we will focus on the new security architecture organizations need to build in order to address the new form of corporate network that is not tethered to a single type of physical network and enables a mobile workforce.

CHAPTER 4

Security Transformation

"*Security is an obvious priority. Without it, the rest of cloud transformation cannot happen.*"

Hervé Coureil, Chief Digital Office, Schneider Electric

Traditional security approaches focused on establishing a perimeter around the corporate network

For over 30 years, IT security focused on protecting an organization by establishing a perimeter to secure the corporate network. This approach was based on the premise that all enterprise users, data, and applications resided on the corporate network. To meet the requirements of this approach, organizations deployed a "castle-and-moat" security approach where the corporate network was the "castle" that was surrounded by a "moat" of security appliances. To allow traffic in and out of the "castle," organizations created internet gateways that provide a drawbridge across the "moat." These gateways initially consisted of a network firewall to establish a physical perimeter separating the internet from users, data, and applications.

As internet traffic increased and cyber attacks became more sophisticated, the "moat" was expanded to include new appliances to form an outbound gateway to enable users to access the internet. This gateway, or DMZ (Demilitarized Zone), was comprised of URL filtering, anti-virus, data loss prevention, and sandbox appliances. In addition to outbound internet gateways, organizations introduced inbound gateways to bring remote users into the corporate network. Inbound gateways generally consist of load balancers, DDoS (Distributed Denial of Service) protection, firewalls, and VPN concentrators. Under the legacy approach, internet and VPN traffic must pass through a DMZ consisting of multiple appliances.

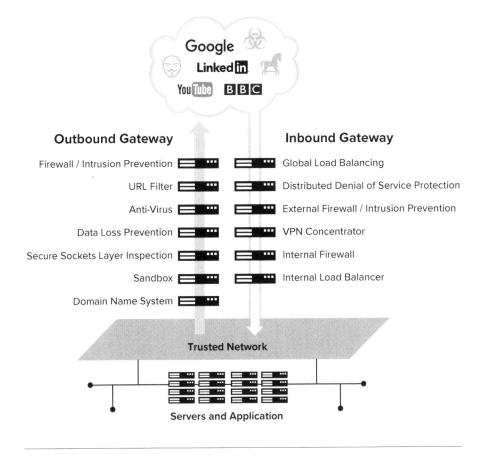

Figure 4.1 Legacy inbound and outbound gateways

Evaluating Castle-and-Moat in the Cloud Era

Your security transformation journey starts with looking at how your castle-and-moat security architecture is run. When users are mobile, working remotely or in branch offices, and the applications they use are in the cloud, routing traffic back across a "hub-and-spoke" network to the data center for access and security controls provides a poor user experience. To deliver a fast user experience, traffic needs to be routed directly to the internet. Routing traffic directly to the internet, while maintaining access and security controls, may require deployment of hundreds, if not thousands, of internet gateways, which would be prohibitively expensive to purchase, deploy, and manage. These appliances are not elastic in nature, as is the case with cloud-native solutions, and tend to have different capabilities at different scales. As such, a solution deployed on premises in the data center will not translate identically for a 100-person branch implementation.

The traditional security model of hub-and-spoke makes the adoption of cloud and mobility extremely costly and cumbersome. It results in organizations having to make decisions that lead to significant tradeoffs:

- **Cost and Complexity:** To maintain a certain level of security and user experience, you will need to deploy top-of-the-line appliances to the hundreds of branches and ensure that they are all kept in sync on policy. Deploying, integrating, and maintaining these gateways, each of which is a collection of heterogeneous network and security appliances with separate management and reporting systems, is resource intensive and complex to manage. This complexity leads to reduced reliability of the networking and security infrastructure.

- **Security tradeoffs:** To keep cost and complexity in check, you will be forced to deploy gear in branches that are less sophisticated than what you have in your data center, and this leads to reduced security efficacy. As the majority of internet traffic is now encrypted, this tradeoff is increasingly risky as organizations often do not have or do not utilize SSL decryption on their appliances and are therefore blind to a large proportion of their traffic. In addition, security appliances come from a heterogeneous array of vendors and are not designed to share threat information, leading to a severe limitation in the level of threat detection and prevention.

- **Poor user experience:** Backhauling traffic through these traditional dedicated Wide Area Network, or WAN, techniques, such as MPLS or leased lines and the serial processing of traffic by network security appliances introduces latency that results in a poor user experience.

In general, applying old security paradigms to a digital enterprise forces the organization to make trade offs. The situation is made even more complex due to the evolving threat landscape as we'll highlight next.

Evolving Threat Landscape

Risks to cybersecurity represent a growing trend for the modern enterprise. Threats are not only more prevalent, they are more impactful, and threat actors grow more sophisticated with their methods of attack. Corporate data breaches are increasing in numbers and a topic of conversation in every board meeting. As such, the tools the cyber security teams use must evolve as the threat actors and threat vectors have evolved.

While security infrastructure has remained static in a state of staid intransigence, malware has evolved:

- **As SSL spreads, so does encrypted malware:** More than 70% of internet traffic is now SSL-delivered, and that percentage will climb.[4] That's a good thing. Such encryption exploits are growing: Over the course of 2017, SSL-encoded malware attacks increased more than 30%.[5] With the coming industry standardization of TLS 1.3, traditional forensic-analysis scanning techniques like packet capture will cease to be effective. With nearly all traffic SSL-delivered, next-generation firewalls will no longer effectively protect corporate netwtorks.

- **Credentials are more easily stolen or corrupted:** Controlling identity is the first line of defense for any corporation in the cloud era. However, most organizations have many identity stores making it easy for hackers to compromise employee identity without knowledge. Complicating matters further, access is often extended to contractors or offsite workers. Keeping identity data current becomes harder when accounts go stale. Furthermore, social-engineering hackers pose a significant threat as they exploit human nature to get at critical corporate assets.

- **BYOD keeps employees happy but opens doors for hackers:** Enterprises must accommodate network access for mobile devices. If those devices are not necessarily company-issued, it's difficult to ensure appropriate device security posture: Many high-profile security breaches and viruses (notably, CryptoLocker) spread laterally after infected devices are brought onto the corporate network.

- **Threats are self-morphing and rapidly evolving:** The now-famous APT1 report, named for an advanced persistent threat team and which described for the first time a concerted hacking campaign emanating from

---

4 February 2018 Zscaler SSL Threat Report: https://www.zscaler.com/blogs/research/february-2018-zscaler-ssl-threat-report
5 ibid.

China, kicked off the shift to so-called breach detection and response.[6] The most recent scourge to appear is ransomware and many organizations have succumbed to debilitating attacks from NotPetya and WannaCry. Today, there can be 100 variants of a new strain of ransomware appearing overnight.

- **Trusted networks lead to lateral attacks:** The modern enterprise cannot secure itself without assuming its walls have already been breached. Attackers these days go to great lengths to ensure they can laterally proliferate an organization in a stealthy manner. Without segmentation and continuously monitoring traffic between employees and applications, and between server-to-server, the enterprise is blind to its threat posture being compromised.

Securing the modern enterprise with a cloud security ecosystem

The key to securing the modern enterprise is to focus directly on securing the data, and much less on securing the network that it resides on. In a world where the organization relies on multiple data center providers, multiple cloud providers, multiple network providers, and to a variety of end computing devices, the data security model starts with classification and appropriate risk treatment and risk acceptance. A new security ecosystem is required to protect enterprise data.

Data Classification and Responsibilities

The transition to a cloud security ecosystem will require organizations to think through the responsibility matrix of their data security needs to determine

---

6 MANDIANT: APT1 report: https://www.fireeye.com/content/dam/fireeye-www/services/pdfs/mandiant-apt1-report.pdf

what can be controlled by the organization and what can be taken as SLAs from their providers.

To secure enterprise data in this new paradigm, one has to classify applications into two basic types: *externally-managed* and *internally-managed*. A parallel is looking at managed versus unmanaged user devices.

Two basic types of applications:

- **Externally-managed:** These are internet destinations or SaaS applications that have their own data security mechanisms that you can neither control nor dictate. Some examples of these are applications such as CNN, Box, and Salesforce.

- **Internally-managed:** These are applications that are hosted in your data center or your IaaS provider for which you ensure data security. Examples of these are an SAP application in your data center, or an employee portal hosted in your AWS instance.

In the legacy world, applications were managed internally, and as such all the responsibility for running, managing, and securing these applications was within the realm of the enterprise. This model, however, fractures when deploying in the cloud. In the new world you enter into a shared responsibility model. For example, with externally managed applications such as Salesforce, you cannot run your own firewall in front of it, nor can you run your own malware engine. In the cloud, you have to create a solution that can augment those services provided by the vendors, with the right levels of control to ensure that the organization leveraged the cloud securely.[7]

---

7 CSA STAR: The Future of Cloud Trust and Assurance https://cloudsecurityalliance.org/star/#_overview

Security Requirements	Responsibility Matrix	
	Legacy World	New World
Identity, Authentication and Authorization	Enterprise	Enterprise
Logging & Security Operations Center (SOC)	Enterprise	Enterprise
Optimized access from any device	Enterprise	Enterprise
Firewalls	Enterprise	Provider & Enterprise
Upgrades	Enterprise	Provider & Enterprise
Malware inspection	Enterprise	Provider & Enterprise
Data Loss Prevention (DLP)	Enterprise	Provider & Enterprise

Table 4.1 Application responsibility matrix

Blueprint for a Cloud Security Ecosystem

Figure 4.2 illustrates an architecture blueprint for a cloud security ecosystem. This ecosystem has to provide all the same functions previously available in the data center, but in a form factor that is no longer tethered to a network.

In the cloud, you don't have a "trusted network" as defined in the on-premises world anymore. Threat assessment and mitigation now have to be done continuously, at different levels, and in real-time. Neil MacDonald from Gartner defines this framework as CARTA (Continuously Assessed Risk/Trust and Adapting).[8] Identity, context-aware policy, and continuous monitoring are the key pillars to Gartner's CARTA and of the cloud security blueprint of the future.

---

8   Zero Trust Is an Initial Step on the Roadmap to CARTA: https://www.gartner.com/document/3895267

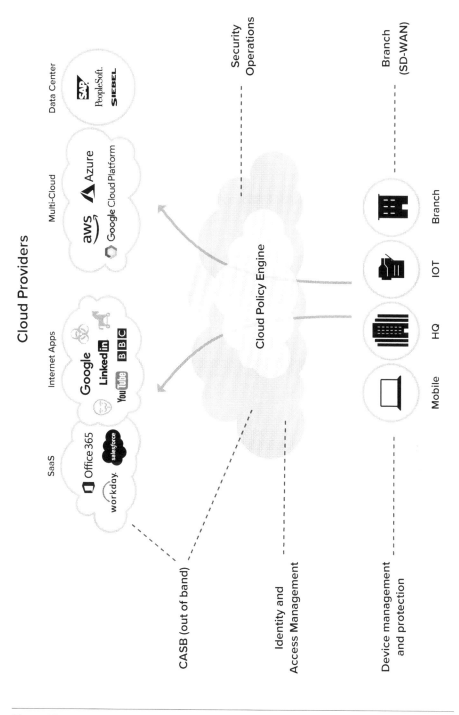

Figure 4.2 A blueprint for the cloud security ecosystem

The following components represent some key requirements of a cloud security ecosystem:

1. Identity and Access Management

As you move to the cloud, defining "trust" parameters and establishing identity are crucial. This critical component becomes the starting point for any secure cloud transformation journey. Having a single aggregation point for federating identity to all applications becomes the first line of defense. The identity management system must be able to provide multi-factor authentication, step-up authentication, and adaptive authentication capabilities. Identity providers can detect potentially malicious or harmful activity based on deviations from the norm. Ideally the identity system is not only providing authentication, but also entitlement and authorization for the use of resources. Authorization is typically done by policy on the gateway. However, this can result in misconfigurations. The application, as well as the access gateway, should feed on the same assertion from the identity provider as the single source of truth. This ensures there are no mismatched firewall rules or orphaned rule lines in the firewall as people, organizations, and roles change over time. The identity provider must become the single point for all permission management.

2. Cloud Policy Engine

The foundation of a cloud security ecosystem is the cloud policy engine that is located at the intersection of all types of network flows—from managed to unmanaged devices and locations, to externally or internally managed clouds. This engine must seamlessly interface with the identity management, software-defined WAN, device management tools, and SOC (Security Operations Center) solutions.

It must be optimally located near the shortest path between the user and the application, and once identity and authorization are established, the connection between the user and the application must be continuously inspected by it. Most identity providers can signal changes in real-time with SCIM (System for Cross-domain Identity Management) if a risk profile changes. The network must be able to take action immediately on the new risk, even on existing sessions.

There are two types of functions the engine must provide depending on whether the destination is internally or externally managed. For externally managed applications, the gateway must provide a complete security inspection stack with capabilities to detect malicious threats using SSL interception, deep packet inspection, IPS, zero-day vulnerability shielding, sandboxing, and machine learning. The engine must also provide full inline data loss prevention to ensure data boundaries as defined by the compliance team can be maintained. For internally managed applications, this policy engine must ensure that the right user or device is getting connected to the right application without exposing your application/server network to the user. Since the policy engine front ends all application access, it must also subsume functions such as local and global load-balancing for continuous availability, and defend against denial of service attacks.

There are several common characteristics that this cloud policy engine must satisfy for this architecture to be effective:

1. It must integrate seamlessly with the identity and entitlement system. For example, it should be able to accept SAML-based authentication and entitlement like your applications do.

2. It must provide the same capabilities regardless of the user location or device type, as well as the location of the destination application.

For example, a branch with five people, an employee at home on an Android phone, and those at the corporate headquarters must have the same (not just similar) security enforcement and user experience capabilities.

3. It must ubiquitously serve all application destinations. For example, the cloud policy engine must be well connected to all clouds, be it AWS, Azure, or Salesforce clouds.

4. It must integrate seamlessly with the existing SOC, governance, and remediation functions. For example, the SOC should have complete visibility within the logging and monitoring systems and be able to complete remediation workflows within their existing toolchains.

3. Security Operations Center (SOC)

The role of a SOC is ever more critical in a cloud-first world, providing a fast path to build and extend your proactive threat hunting capabilities. Unlike the on-premise world where the scope of monitoring the data center was limited to having control and visibility of the data alone, in the cloud, user and device mobility compounded by a complex and evolving threat environment require a much more sophisticated approach.

Organizations must always assume the posture of being compromised and ensure they have continuous, real-time visibility of all activities on the network, the endpoints, and their cloud applications in place. This requires integrating logs from all relevant inputs and correlating them with internal and external threat intelligence to ensure that any breach is detected and curtailed in the shortest time possible.

However, due to the amount of data that traverses the enterprise today, it is crucial to have tools in place that summarize the organizational risk by automatically classifying incidents and events into priorities for the SOC to follow up.

4. Cloud Access Security Broker (CASB)

In the legacy world, organizations deployed tools such as RSA Archer to ensure access controls were correctly set up and regularly audited. There were also malware inspection engines running on the application host itself, and protections such as web application firewalls (WAF) to prevent application level attacks.

With SaaS applications, these controls must be augmented through a CASB platform. Gartner defines a CASB as security policy enforcement points placed between cloud service consumers and cloud service providers to combine and interject enterprise security policies as the cloud-based resources are accessed.[9] CASBs consolidate multiple types of security policy enforcement—authentication, single sign-on, authorization, credential mapping, device profiling, encryption, tokenization, and so on.

CASB deployment modes are broadly categorized into the following two categories: *Inline* and *Out-of-band*.

1. Cloud-native policy engines already support inline CASB capabilities. This provides most of the CASB functionality for an organization as all traffic of all users should be flowing through it before any cloud application is accessed.

---

9 Gartner: Cloud Access Security Brokers (CASBs) https://www.gartner.com/it-glossary/cloud-access-security-brokers-casbs/

2. For traffic that cannot pass through a cloud policy engine or cannot be inspected by this engine, an out-of-band service is required that ensures the security of the data that has been hosted in the externally or internally managed application also known as an out-of-band cloud access security broker (API-CASB). An API-CASB can also help monitor and control flows that may move data from cloud to cloud without any user interaction.

5. Data Privacy and Compliance

When you use Salesforce or Office 365 your data—your content—is stored in the cloud: Salesforce has your records and Office 365 has your email and files, so you need to protect your data. On the other hand, a cloud security service that provides secure access to the internet and SaaS is a security checkpoint function—it should not be storing content at all. Pages visited are inspected but no content is stored. Only logs are stored. It's almost like an international airport. Your baggage goes through an x-ray machine and, once it is scanned and no threat is identified, your luggage is approved for transportation. No copy of its content is kept. It's critical that your logs are stored in a location of your choice and obfuscated in a way to satisfy local compliance requirements.

With scores of checkposts around the internet, you would find yourself with a problem if logs were written in every data center, as they would be scattered and may not be protected. While logs do not store content or data, they still have user-identifiable information such as user ID, IP address, or machine identifiers. Ideally, a good cloud security service would not write logs locally but write once to a location of the customer's choice. An EU company should have the option to store logs in the EU, just as U.S. companies should be able to store logs in the U.S. Large companies may want to store their logs in their own data center.

Some traditional security checkposts do content caching for performance improvement, which means they may store content locally. This increases the data security risk, as the customer data may reside in various data centers. For this reason, a good security service should not cache content, especially since it offers little value in this day of dynamic content.

With proper, customer-defined storage, it would be easier to be compliant with GDPR, but only if the architecture is done right.

There are 111 countries around the world that have passed data privacy laws. The EU General Data Protection Regulation (EU GDPR) is the latest and arguably the most impactful of these. Every organization that collects or even processes data on EU residents will have to prove compliance. This may include employing a special data protection officer (DPO) whose job is to communicate with the data protection supervisor in each country. Noncompliance with GDPR exposes an organization to hefty fines of 20 million euros or four percent of global revenue, whichever is greater.

Benefits of a cloud security platform

The pioneers of this cloud security transformation have all realized these benefits.

Cost savings. Savings are possible just from the reduction in backhaul expense over MPLS circuits. Canceling or avoiding the subscription and maintenance contracts for unified threat management appliances is another major cost savings. The cost of managing hundreds of devices, either by internal teams or an MSSP (Managed Service Security Provider), are also avoided. Factor in the elimination of the need to reinvest in capital equipment every five years or so and the cost arguments get even better.

Enhanced user experience. Going directly to the internet from any location invariably leads to better performance of web applications. The contributors to this book all report positive impacts on the user experience. In the future, as available internet connection speeds grow, especially with the impending move to 5G networks, everyone's experience will only improve.

Better security. Consistently applied policies and protections no matter the device or location is the secret to good security. A cloud service provider takes advantage of scale to deliver those protections sooner. Millions of endpoints being targeted by threat actors means the cloud service will detect new attacks or malicious URLs early and automatically update the protections for all users.

AutoNation

Embracing a New Security Architecture for Access to Internet and SaaS Applications

Company:	**AutoNation**	Revenue:	**$122 billion**
Sector:	**Retail**	Employees:	**28,000**
Driver:	**Ken Athanasiou**	Countries:	**1**
Role:	**CISO**	Locations:	**300**

Company IT Footprint: AutoNation has approximately 28,000 employees. It is the largest seller of cars in the United States. They have 300+ locations with internet points of presence.

"When ransomware attacks happen to other companies, thousands of systems in their environment are crippled, in addition to having serious impacts with having to pay a ransom. When this kind of event hits the news, I get worried calls from executives, and it warms my heart to be able to tell them, 'We're fine.'"

Ken Athanasiou, VP and Chief Information Security Officer, AutoNation

---

AutoNation is a retail organization with 300 locations selling and servicing automobiles. Ken Athanasiou, Chief Information Security Officer at AutoNation, describes how cloud transformation saved them money while enabling new capabilities. He stresses the importance of timing and careful planning when embarking on a major strategic initiative such as cloud transformation. He further expands on the importance of being adaptable organizationally, and the willingness to make modifications to plans along the way, and approaching it with more of an agile methodology to prevent false starts and failures.

In the words of Ken Athanasiou:

Flexibility, repeatability, and security through cloud transformation

I've been at AutoNation for a little over three and a half years, as its first CISO. AutoNation has about 28,000 employees and we are the largest seller of cars in the United States. Prior to joining AutoNation, I was at American Eagle Outfitters as their CISO for about seven years. Previously I was at JPMorgan Chase, as the retail line-of-business information security officer, or BISO, for five years.

Journey begins with a breach

AutoNation experienced a small breach with a third-party vendor in 2014 that exposed about 1,800 customer records. That was enough for our general counsel to start asking questions about ways to improve security. He and a few other executives brought in a couple of different firms to do some assessments and make some recommendations, and one of those recommendations was to build out an independent cyber security team that could help them reduce the risks.

Closing the digital divide

At the same time, there was beginning to be a digital divide, especially for the customers. There is also a digital divide between the brick-and-mortar stores where vehicles are sold and our online presence. The intent is to close that divide and present to our customers a comprehensive user experience, where they can begin the shopping, selection, and credit application process online. They can wander into a store, access what they did online, and move the process forward a few steps; they can then go home, make a few decisions, sleep on it, whatever, and then either complete the purchase process online or come into the store the next day.

Closing that digital gap and giving our customers the opportunity to participate in a unique buying experience has become a driver for this organization.

Protecting customer data

There are unique security challenges to being an online auto dealer. We take credit applications every day, and credit applications are obviously about the most sensitive personally identifiable information (PII) that you can handle. We also process credit card transactions, so we deal with PCI requirements.

"We're extremely paranoid about how we handle our customers' data."

When we have a credit application, we have every piece of information that a bad guy needs to do some pretty robust identity-theft activities, so we're extremely paranoid about how we handle our customers' data. A critical element of this process is the ability to protect that type of data, while allowing customers to access it.

Transitioning the CIO

I was hired by a new CIO who had joined the organization just a few months before I did. He was brought in to do some transformational activity and had inherited a significant amount of technology debt within the organization. We made some progress under that CIO and did an enormous amount of work around solving some of that technology debt and getting security in place—and closing some of the most critical gaps that the organization had.

Over the last year and a half or so, we've made some dramatic changes within the technology organization. We've been able to advance the maturity of the process, get completeness, and instill some robust frameworks.

Backing off on cloud backups

The decision to move to the cloud was made by the technology operations team with our disaster recovery (DR) capability. The misstep we made was to take legacy applications that were heavily dependent upon very large hulking boxes of iron that run very hot and heavy and putting them into a cloud environment without actually refactoring those applications.

The transition didn't go well. We were about four months late exiting the data center and six months late in actually executing a test against the new cloud DR environment. As predicted, that test failed miserably. We had transactions that had been sub-second go to 60+ seconds from the physical colocation to the cloud environment. It was an abject failure.

One of the first conversations I had with the new technology lead was about fixing our DR environment. We needed to fix it fast, and we had a discussion about what's the right thing to do. Do we refactor these applications so that they can play well in the cloud? After some discussions with the application development teams, we determined it would take us approximately two to three years to fully refactor the applications, based on the available resources, the workload, and the business requirements.

We made a decision as a team at that stage that the organization could not suffer that type of risk for such an extended period of time. The executives agreed with us and we built a new colo data center. Brand new hardware, all sorts of beautiful, shiny new toys in that data center, and we moved all those applications out of the cloud, back into the traditional data center.

Timing is everything

Although the decision to go to the cloud was a wonderful idea, the problem was that the time frame associated with doing that transition and the requirements of actually executing that transition weren't fully understood.

As with anything, if you don't truly understand what you need to do, you're likely to fail at it. Unless you are adaptable, and you are willing to make modifications to your plans along the way, and approach it with more of an agile methodology, you will fail.

Embracing cloud security

On the client application side, one of the other things that I did when I first got to AutoNation was to install UTM (unified threat management) devices; these are basically SOHO, small home office types of appliances, that combine all the features and functionality of the next-gen firewall on a very small platform.

We had 300+ locations with internet points of presence. The networking team was intending to deploy more than 300 little boxes across the entire country and that's when I decided it was time for us to learn more about this cool cloud-based network firewall solution that I'd heard of called Zscaler. That's when I called up Jay and his team and asked to meet with them.

Instead of doing the little boxes of iron across the entire country and rolling trucks all over the place and having to manage that nightmare architecture, we went down the Zscaler route, which was intense. I didn't sleep for probably six months. I was worried about our exposure. Every time I went to bed, I expected to wake up to a major breach until we got Zscaler rolled out across the environment.

Addressing the security debt

There were quite a few issues that we uncovered as soon as we wrapped Zscaler as a prophylactic around the environment—lack of robust patching and IT hygiene, the ineffectiveness of the McAfee antivirus that we were running, broken update processes across the board, very old systems, middleware that wasn't being patched.

We looked at various engines that were out there, including hardware based. Three years ago, there really wasn't any other cloud-based solution that was even comparable to the capabilities that Zscaler had. They were the only true, full-protocol firewall in the cloud. They had the most robust capabilities. Everything else was pretty much just a web proxy. You can pump your traffic through that, but it's definitely not the same thing.

The rollout decision was a no-brainer

Zscaler was just a completely different architecture, so we made the decision to pilot Zscaler and see how it looked and felt. We rolled out Zscaler to a couple of stores and our corporate headquarters and we let that run for a little bit. Again, the visibility we got into outbound bot traffic, and obvious infections and those sorts of things very quickly upped the urgency of getting a solution deployed across the entire environment.

It became pretty much a no-brainer, and we made the decision to go forward with this even if we had to break a bunch of stuff in order to filter traffic and gain control. We invested capital to drive some maturity into our patching processes and to improve our anti-malware controls.

We took advantage of Zscaler's anti-malware. When I was first talking with the Zscaler team, I was adamant that I wanted full-blown next-gen firewall capabilities, which would include filtering network-based malware detection and sandboxing.

We are now pretty much fully deployed with Zscaler capabilities. We're currently not making extensive use of their Zscaler Private Access to access our internal applications, although it's compelling. We just simply haven't had the opportunity to really push that out very far. But we've got pretty much everything else, like DLP, and all the obvious stuff around the URL filtering. We are now a heavy consumer of Zscaler capabilities and we've been very pleased with the controls that we got from them.

Penetration testing has become more difficult, and that's a good thing

We do aggressive penetration testing using third-party vendors. It's common for them to become stymied by the Zscaler layer when they're doing remote testing, because they simply can't penetrate the malware and sandboxing controls and get anything to work. That's also a result of the changes that we've made around patching. We're using Tanium for end-point management across our entire environment, which I am just in love with—it's a fantastic piece of technology.

So, with all these additional controls in place and obviously driving mature patch processes throughout our environment, our resiliency—our hardness, so to speak—has just gone several levels above where we were previously.

Seeing is believing: The value of reporting

For reporting we don't often use the stock stuff that comes out of Zscaler, but we do pull numbers from it to include in board presentations. I show the board a bunch of gee-whiz numbers, and these gee-whiz numbers show for the most part how much we're under attack. The reason I call these gee-whiz numbers is because every single one of these attacks was blocked or prevented by one of the engines that we have in place. This particular set of numbers shows all the attacks or incidents that were blocked or prevented by our cloud-based firewall solution, Zscaler.

It's more of a validation that this is stuff that we would have to deal with if we didn't have these controls in place, but the fact is, we do have these controls and, therefore, we wouldn't consider these incidents or really anything all that important to deal with. We don't react to them because they're noise that is filtered out by the engines that we have in place.

The senior executive staff loves the numbers, because they look at them and they go, "Holy smokes, that's a lot!" Every now and again, we do see spikes in attack activity and I usually end up having to explain the spikes. "What happened there where it jumped up so high?" they'll ask, and then I'll usually explain how there is a zero-day exploit or a critical vulnerability that was discovered and we see an enormous amount of traffic attacking that critical vulnerability because it was fresh and new.

"We're fine"

When ransomware attacks happen to other companies, thousands of systems in their environment are crippled, in addition to having serious impacts with having to pay a ransom. When this kind of event hits the news, I get worried calls from executives, and it warms my heart to be able to tell them, "We're fine."

We've gotten down to a seven-day patch cycle, and that's not even a critical or an urgent cycle. If we have a critical patch that needs to be pushed, we can do that in about 24-hours.

Piloting the types of engines that can give visibility into the state of your environment, like the level of botnet traffic and infections, is something that you can then use to drive further activity, spending, and resource implementation.

It's important to really understand what is going on in your environment in terms of infections and risk levels in order to put something like Zscaler in place. For example, if you have 70 infections, you will find that maybe your patch processes are broken. Then, you could start piloting a couple of engines that look at EDR, response, and software distribution packages. Do a side-by-side comparison, and you'll find that your Microsoft SCCM product says you're fully patched—but then when you run something that's independent of Microsoft against that, it says you're only patched at about 50%. Well, in that case, you've got things in your environment that are missing patches, that are two years old, so something's wrong there. Again, that would drive further activity to resolve.

Our Office 365 implementation needed more bandwidth at each point of presence

As we made the transition to Office 365, we had to learn how to implement the process. Originally, we were going to have everybody use the portal and not bother putting Office on individual machines. Also, we didn't have the required bandwidth. It didn't work, so we had to step back and change up how we do things as a process. Now we're doing local installs of Office 365, and we're executing the product differently. It works much better now.

At the time, every one of our locations had from a T-1 up to a multiple T-1 type of MPLS connections back to our data center, so very small pipes for the private circuit back to the data center.

Internet access was also not all that great. You're talking somewhere around ten megabits per second type of connections to the internet, which, obviously, if you're not careful with that type of an environment, you will easily clog those pipes and you will have very degraded performance.

Local internet breakouts helped reduce costs

After we got the new technology leadership in place, we renegotiated with our providers and we significantly reduced our network bandwidth cost and jacked up our bandwidth ten-fold. We went from very small MPLS circuits to ten and 20 megabits per second MPLS circuits back to our data center, and 150 megabits per second connections to the internet for the most part. We had very significant increases in performance and capability for internet bandwidth, and again, that was primarily due to a technology gap, lack of planning, and a lack of understanding of the bandwidth requirements involving our most used applications. We still do have MPLS circuits and we have internet circuits. The vast majority of our traffic goes direct to the internet, but we do have internal applications, like our CRM and some other systems, that we just simply backhaul across the MPLS circuit.

Today, we are still using a hybrid network. We have considered doing away with those MPLS circuits and going full internet, maybe using things like a ZPA, but we've not made that transition at this point.

We don't use Zscaler for mobile devices at this point. That's another one of those things that's on the list, but we have not actually executed against it. We're transitioning from Intune over to AirWatch right now for MDM, and once we complete that, we'll go back and look at what else we could do in that space.

Improving the user experience

One of the other advantages that we've gotten out of Zscaler for some of our other cloud-based applications is that the connection speeds through Zscaler are actually pretty robust. This goes back to the peering that Zscaler has done with a lot of the other larger providers out there, like with Microsoft and Office 365. Our number of hops—even though we have to do a tunnel from our external router into the nearest Zscaler cloud, and from Zscaler to Office 365—is only one or two hops, versus going directly from our dealership to the internet; it would actually take longer to get to the service than going through Zscaler.

Instead of inducing additional latency because of those pairing connections, we get all our controls in place and we see very minimal latency and, in some cases, our connections are actually even faster.

Taking advantage of cloud capabilities

There are multiple inherent advantages of moving to the cloud. You get better resiliency, you get better scalability, you get a lot of really cool abilities that you can't get out of a standard colo environment, and as you re-architect your legacy applications, as you build new applications so that they're actually cloud-focused and can natively take advantage of those capabilities, I expect that we will continue to see more and more of these applications move into this model.

Another advantage is in mergers and acquisitions. For M&A, Zscaler has been a big win for us. When we do acquisitions or divestitures, it's very easy to enroll a new location in our environment. We don't have to roll a piece of security hardware out there. For the acquired entity, we simply configure the tunnels for the internet bound traffic to Zscaler and we're covered.

One of the things that we've found to be a little interesting is when we divest a dealership, the acquirer comes in, and they may ask us what we do for our network security. They ask us where our firewall is located. Our response to that has been—we use Zscaler, so you don't have a physical firewall in there. You're going to have to figure something out. They don't like that answer because they're used to just taking whatever was there and making use of it.

"When we do acquisitions or divestitures, it's very easy to enroll a new location in our environment."

When we do an acquisition, we do more of a rip-and-replace for the technology environment. We may purchase computers with an acquisition, but then we generally will rip them out. We'll resell them to someone else and put our stuff in.

MAN Energy Solutions

Ensuring Both Internal and External Application Access with a Cloud Security Architecture

Company:	MAN Energy Solutions	Revenue:	$4.3 billion
Type:	Manufacturing	Employees:	15,000
Driver:	Tony Fergusson	Countries:	6
Role:	IT Infrastructure Architect	Locations:	100

Company IT Footprint: MAN Energy Solutions has 15,000 people in over 100 locations. They have fleets of engines on ships deployed all over the world. Their main offices are in Germany and Denmark. This entity is actually part of the Volkswagen Group, so they are a part of a larger 650,000 person organization.

"To be successful, you really need to sell this concept of cloud transformation—you need to evolve the organizational mindset. This technology is so disruptive that you need the people inside your company onboard."

Tony Fergusson, IT Infrastructure Architect, MAN Energy Solutions

---

MAN Energy Solutions is a manufacturer of large engines and turbines with fleets of engines on ships deployed all over the world. Tony Fergusson wanted to move to a model where internal applications were not even visible to attackers. Only authenticated users can see them. He calls this stealth approach the "black cloud," and they use the concept to securely access engine sensors on their deployed fleet. He shares how they truly discovered the flexibility of cloud-delivered security when they had their first experiences with ransomware—thanks to their cloud security service, this was a non-event.

In the words of Tony Fergusson:

Eight years ago, we started our journey to the cloud at MAN Energy Solutions when I went down the path of creating a forward proxy for access to the internet. I have been in the IT industry for over 20 years. I started with IBM in 1995, so really at the beginning of the internet. I worked at an application service provider (ASP) back in New Zealand, kind of the precursor for what the cloud is today. I have been working in Europe for ten years, mostly in Denmark for MAN Energy Solutions. While a lot of my experience is with Microsoft products like SharePoint and Office 365, I am actually a network architect.

Moving to cloud-based proxies for internet and SaaS applications

Our on-premises proxy gateways needed to be replaced, so I went to the market and discovered Zscaler for secure internet access. At the time, 2011, they were very new. Now I can say we have been a long-term customer.

> "We saw that the future was direct access to the internet from everywhere, while at the same time, we needed to inspect all that traffic."

Back then, we backhauled all internet traffic from every location and had one connection to the internet. We saw that the future was direct access to the internet from everywhere, while at the same time, we needed to inspect all that traffic. As a result, over several years, we went to local breakouts everywhere and inspection of all traffic in the Zscaler cloud security platform. From a security perspective, this model has been a huge success for our company. We discovered the flexibility of cloud-delivered security when we had our first experiences with ransomware. We simply enabled Zscaler sandboxing for all of our users and the problem went away.

Secure access to internal data center applications without VPN

Back in 2014, I had a lot of discussions with Zscaler around what I call "black cloud"; the whole idea was that my applications should not even be visible to attackers. In 2015, we started beta testing Zscaler Private Access (ZPA). We first used it for the many consultants we work with around the world. Our old system of VPNs was very hard to manage. It was difficult to onboard people and get the visibility into what they were accessing.

The first proof-of-concept (PoC) with ZPA was to onboard consultants and it was very successful. We quickly brought all of our consultants onto the platform and we went into full production in 2016, going live in April, the same date that Zscaler officially launched the product. That was when it dawned on me just how powerful this solution was, and we could really do a lot with this technology.

Secure access to engine applications in large ships

The next use case was to start looking at protecting our engines deployed in all of our seagoing vessels. There were only certain people that should be allowed access to the control systems and monitoring software on those vessels so we deployed ZPA.

One of the interesting things about ZPA is that it fulfills my vision of the black cloud. Basically, ZPA acts as a broker for connections. The client software does not know the IP address of the end system. A request is sent and if the requester is properly identified and authorized to get access to the application—or, in this case, the software running on the engine management platform—ZPA initiates the session. It's like the call-back setting on modems back in the day. The whole platform is based on DNS, so you essentially extract the whole network from the equation. Before ZPA, we were assigning a class-C network space to each engine on every ship. With ZPA, we basically created a namespace routing in between us and the customer. This allowed us to monitor hundreds of ships without looking for a new IP address range.

Now we can secure each connection, which we can define per user per application. We have access control to each engine and we could add strong authentication through identity federation. That led to a thought—why not just replace all of our VPNs with ZPA for all users? After taking that step, it became quite apparent that the next step was to determine what our corporate wide area network was for and if we even needed a corporate network. Why not just put everyone on the internet and secure the access through some sort of software-defined perimeter?

Certainly, we are not there yet but I think within the next few years we will be. Look at WannaCry and NotPetya. Making the corporate campus one big open network is a mistake. In the past, if users wanted access to unsanctioned things we could not support, we just told them no. Now we tell them if you want access to those applications, you have to go through the Zscaler fabric.

We're starting to migrate applications to AWS, and we have to deploy connectors up there, so we'll get connectivity for people to access them. I think of it as the company making its own black cloud. I don't care where the user is or what device they are on. I don't care whether you are at the office or at home. I just need you to get to the application. If you go through this secure fabric, I know who you are and I know that you actually should have access to this app.

This is the top priority model I have been creating for the company. It is a complete shift in thinking and has taken a couple of years to even solidify it in my head.

Securing the Internet of Things

The biggest problem with IoT is that these devices are generally not patched. They are not complying with standards. They are a security risk. What we are doing is putting this secure fabric between the people who need to access them and the IoT devices themselves.

To accomplish this, we found we needed to create a DNS naming structure. Now our policy is set by DNS names, not IP addresses. I can have an A Record for a device and several different CNAMES, and I can apply policy based on these. The DNS becomes my policy catalog and manager. There is still a lot of thinking we have to do about what this all means.

Better security against ransomware

I remember my management coming to talk to me after NotPetya did so much damage to Maersk. Management was rightfully very concerned. I just looked at them and said, "We're OK. Everything is closed. Every client is closed. We closed the firewalls to everything. The only way you can get to one of our engines is through Zscaler, through this black cloud. So everything is black. The malware has nowhere to go."

Cloud security for integrating M&A

Think about how this fabric applies during M&A. We did one acquisition in Zurich and to onboard the new company, I just gave everyone the Zscaler client. As soon as they had Zscaler Internet Access (ZIA), they were at the same security level as we were. Then, when they got Zscaler Private Access (ZPA) they could access our private apps. The whole process took just two weeks.

Advice to infrastructure leaders

To be successful, you really need to sell this concept of cloud transformation—you need to evolve the organizational mindset. This technology is so innovative that you need the people inside your company onboard. I spent a huge amount of time internally evangelizing to my CSO, my management, and everyone on why this is different, and why this works. To further validate, I pointed to them why I was confident that we were protected, and was able to reassure them when they came down to me worried about NotPetya.

Because of this technology, I was able to call a halt to a big 802.1x project we had been working on for Network Access Control (NAC). NAC does nothing for me when I go home or on the road. On the contrary, it can authorize someone infected with NotPetya to get on the network and the next thing you know, everyone is infected.

What not to do

Don't allow people to build direct IP connectivity into their applications. I wish I had acted earlier to keep that from happening. Get your application developers onboard earlier in the project cycle so they understand the new architecture.

Chapter 4 Takeaways

In a cloud-first world there are no physical boundaries. Controls are enforced by software and networks are taken out of the equation. It is all about users and applications.

Some considerations:

- Castle-and-moat architectures for securing the network are no longer relevant. Provide the right users access to the right applications irrespective of the network, location, or device.

- A built-for-the-cloud security layer is an enabler for cloud transformation. Taking advantage of cloud delivered applications from any device and any location requires distributed security.

- Unlike most security improvements, cloud delivered security enhances user experience.

- Focus on risk. Start with the risks to your data, and evolve to a corporate risk appetite informed by knowledge of threat actors and exposure.

- The burden on IT security teams is lightened, freeing resources to focus on internal security, countering targeted attacks and malicious insiders.

In the next section, we highlight a practical reference architecture for secure cloud transformation and steps taken by one large enterprise organization through their journey.

PRACTICAL CONSIDERATIONS

Chapter 5: Successfully Deploying Office 365

In this chapter we'll highlight some practical enterprise considerations when deploying Office 365, and walk through common challenges and best practices to ensure a successful deployment.

Chapter 6: A Reference Architecture for Secure Cloud Transformation

In this chapter we introduce a reference architecture modeled from a real-world cloud transformation journey, and highlight the stages of transformation and strategies deployed within.

Chapter 7: Perspectives of Leading Cloud Providers

We focus on the evolution of cloud delivered applications through the stories of the dominant cloud platforms, Microsoft Azure, Amazon Web Services, and Google Cloud Platform, and provide tips on selecting the right service for your application needs.

CHAPTER 5

Successfully Deploying Office 365

> *"Office 365 gives us more features, lower cost, and more capability like OneDrive and Teams."*
>
> **Alex Philips, Chief Information Officer, National Oilwell Varco**

Email is still the killer application of the digital age. Companies like Hotmail, Yahoo!, and Google rode the crest of the email wave for consumers while Lotus and Microsoft battled for dominance in the enterprise. Microsoft won the enterprise battle, hands down, with Outlook penetrating most organizations as the standard email client and Microsoft Exchange Server the primary email server.

Microsoft also dominates in the world of client software for office productivity with the Microsoft Office Suite including Word, Excel, and PowerPoint. The other tech giants, Apple and Google in particular, have their eye on Microsoft's markets and Google challenged Microsoft directly when, in 2006, it introduced G Suite, a collection of tools that were completely cloud based and paid for by subscription. G Suite had all the advantages of SaaS: always updated, always backed up, and easy to collaborate within the platform, but it lacked many of the advanced features required by power users.

Being the incumbent in practically every business and government agency in the world, Microsoft had time to transition to the cloud, but they needed to move quickly and it wasn't going to be easy. New leaders are born when mega-shifts take place and few companies have been able to successfully pivot. Microsoft is one of those few companies and Office 365 is a result of their cloud journey.

Microsoft's response to G Suite is Office 365, introduced June 28, 2011, and it is changing the landscape of information technology in the enterprise. Over 70% of the Fortune 500 have already transitioned to Office 365. By the fourth quarter of 2017, revenue from Office 365 surpassed that of the traditional Microsoft Office products. Revenue from Office 365 is growing at 40% percent a year while the number of seats is growing at 28%. The number of monthly active users for Office 365 is 135 million commercial users and 30.6 million consumers (Q3, FY2018).

As enterprises make the transition to Office 365, they are faced with challenges, both from a networking perspective and a security stance.

Why are enterprises adopting Office 365?

Like other SaaS applications, Office 365 has a compelling business case. It includes the combined functionality of email, file sharing, video and voice conferencing, and storage, all with no servers, hardware, networking, or layered-in security products in a data center.

- **Lower total cost of ownership (TCO).** Factor in all the costs associated with maintaining applications, updating them whenever there are new patches available, writing the complicated firewall policies so they work across the corporate network, providing disaster recovery, and scaling the server hardware to accommodate growth.

- **Familiar User Experience.** Office 365 provides a familiar user interface to a generation of office workers who have used Outlook. Very little training is required to make the transition. The other features such as Yammer, SharePoint, Calendar, and Skype for Business are easy to find and use.

- **Integrated functionality.** As an SaaS offering, it is easy for Microsoft to integrate functions in Office 365. The APIs, data structures, and backend processing needed to do this are transparent to your IT staff. It is not their responsibility.

- **Frequent enhancements.** Microsoft can acquire new companies, such as Yammer, and quickly add its functionality to the Office 365 platform.

- **Future-proof.** The pace of new feature additions gives a customer confidence that future capabilities will be introduced in a timely manner.

- **Elastic.** The underlying architecture is maintained by Microsoft, so growth in email volume, or an increasing number of Skype users, should not impact performance.

The fast adoption rates of Office 365 are the best indicator that Microsoft is doing something right. But what are some of the issues with transitioning to Office 365?

Challenges Office 365 creates for enterprise

Office 365 is one of the primary applications driving network transformation. It has unique challenges that must be addressed with special routing, security, and bandwidth optimization.

The number one challenge of migrating to Office 365 is providing a seamless user experience. How users access Office 365 will define their experience. If you have a traditional hub-and-spoke network architecture, you are probably backhauling all your Office 365 traffic from remote branches or users, either over MPLS or a VPN. Then that traffic is routed out from your data center to Microsoft Azure. This architecture lends itself to delivering a less than optimal experience and is the driving factor for Microsoft's recommendation of a direct-to-cloud connection.

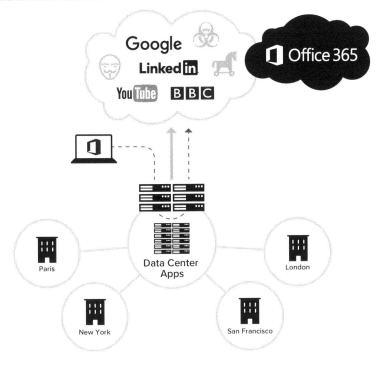

Figure 5.1 Legacy hub-and-spoke is the wrong approach with Office 365

When Kelly Services transitioned to Office 365, they sent Office 365 traffic directly over the internet to each branch. They soon found that they needed to maintain over 700 rules in each of their branch and data center firewalls to ensure Skype for Business worked. If Microsoft adds or updates IP addresses as it expands its cloud infrastructure, all of those rules in all of those branch firewalls in every location will have to be updated quickly, or the service will be impacted.

"Office 365 is one of the primary applications driving network transformation. It has unique challenges that must be addressed with special routing, security, and bandwidth optimization."

Office 365 can be used to replace many desktop applications such as Outlook and the Microsoft Office suite. These productivity applications are different from a typical SaaS product. They need an open state with persistent connections, but typical web proxies, load balancers, and firewalls between the user and Microsoft Azure are traditionally set to time-out inactive TCP/IP sessions, often in less than two minutes. This can lead to productivity problems such as hung sessions, which should be addressed by setting longer session times for Office 365 traffic. That means that as many as 12 to 20 sessions are open in the firewalls for each user, which can quickly add up and potentially surpass the firewall's ability to maintain state.

Because of these issues, Microsoft has provided its guidance to improve user experience with Office 365, published in its Office 365 Enterprise documentation.[10]

10 Office 365 Network Connectivity Principles https://docs.microsoft.com/en-us/office365/enterprise/office-365-network-connectivity-principles

1. Differentiate traffic meant for Office 365 by destination IP address and route it from the user's location. In other words, do not backhaul Office 365 traffic to a hub over MPLS.

2. Provide local DNS (Domain Name System) because the corporate DNS may be in a different geographic region and force the user to connect to a distant Office 365 node. Or, they connect to a local node but their traffic first flows to the corporate servers.

3. Avoid network hairpinning and optimize direct connectivity. The goal is to get to Microsoft's Office 365 infrastructure as directly as possible with the fewest number of hops.

How to deploy Office 365 successfully?

There are three steps required to successfully transition to Office 365. They are the basis of cloud transformation.

Step 1. Secure local internet breakouts

The first step for most organizations is to fix the network. This means a consistent way of getting from a user's device to Office 365. The most efficient way is to go direct-to-cloud. This is initially accomplished with local internet breakouts for Office 365 and other SaaS applications and internet destinations.

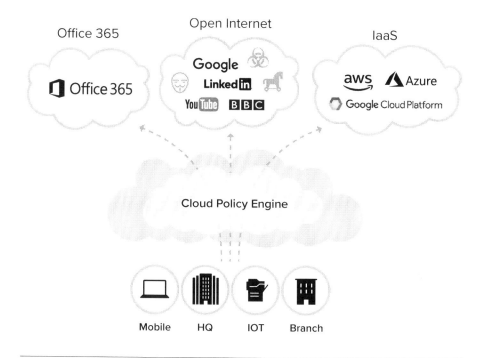

Figure 5.2 Direct-to-cloud: secure local internet breakouts across all locations for every user

Local internet breakouts come with a security burden. To address those issues, connecting through a secure cloud service is required. That connection not only saves from deploying a bunch of security appliance hardware or spinning up VMs all over the place, it happens to solve the issue with the hundreds of ports and policies required for Office 365 to work. The secure cloud service maintains those rules for all of its customers and updates them in real time. From the branch office or data center, you just need a simple set of rules that directs Office 365 (and internet) traffic to the nearest node of the secure cloud service.

Step 2. Local DNS for Office 365

Often overlooked when deploying local internet breakouts is DNS. You may have issues if you maintain DNS back in the data center. Even though users are going directly to the internet, they have to wait while their DNS requests make that hairpin detour. A DNS server located in another region may not provide the optimal IP address and people in a remote region may find they are accessing Office 365 in a Microsoft data center that is far removed from them. While traditional security appliances were never designed to resolve DNS, it's imperative that the cloud security service offer DNS resolution or can override DNS to provide a local connection.

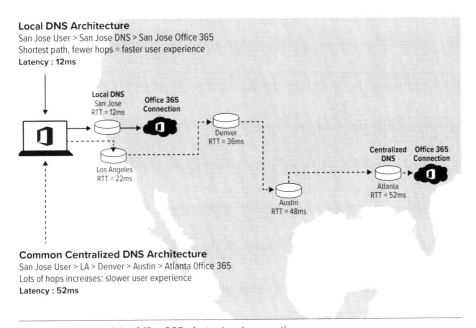

Figure 5.3 Local DNS for Office 365—faster local connections

Step 3. Bandwidth allocation and prioritization for Office 365

When Kelly Services, a large workforce augmentation company, re-architected its network to accommodate local internet breakouts for 870 locations, the company determined that it should have a minimum 256 Kbps upload speed per user in each office. This would ensure that the Office 365 collaboration features would work smoothly. A simple metric can help you size the broadband connectivity you will need. An office of thousands of people may need multiple broadband connections.

The significant cost savings which result from reducing the number of MPLS circuits can fund the acquisition of higher broadband speeds. On top of that, replacing security devices at remote offices will reduce how much you pay a managed security service provider or your internal costs for managing those devices.

With direct-to-cloud connections over broadband to a security service you can now deliver a consistent user experience regardless of where the user is connected—at the branch office, headquarters, or even a coffee shop.

While local breakouts help enhance the user experience, you may find that when users are watching YouTube videos or sports events online, Office 365 performance may suffer. There are two reasons for this: a) streaming applications such as YouTube tend to subsume all the available bandwidth; b) the last mile tends to be the bandwidth bottleneck. To mitigate this, cloud security services that sit before the last mile can be leveraged for bandwidth shaping by application class, and to allocate higher bandwidth to mission-critical business applications over the internet. A typical bandwidth policy is to set the Office 365 traffic at 40% of the available bandwidth for a given location. More importantly, Office 365 should be throttled at an upper bound, say 50%, to prevent a OneDrive sync from bringing down the network.

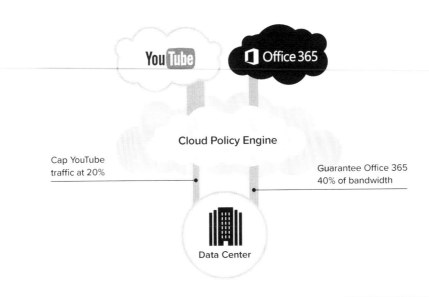

Figure 5.4 Prioritizing Office 365 over other applications on local internet connections

National Oilwell Varco

Office 365 Migration at Scale

Company:	National Oilwell Varco	Revenue:	$7.3 billion
Sector:	Oil and Gas Manufacturing	Employees:	25,000 computer users
Driver:	Alex Philips	Countries:	65
Role:	CIO	Locations:	over 600

Company IT Footprint: National Oilwell Varco is a globally distributed company with plants or operations in over 600 locations. Of their large computing workforce of 25,000 employees, 70% are mobile with laptops.

"Forced by necessity, we had to figure out how to embark on our own journey to modernize and adopt new technology to our business."

Alex Philips, Chief Information Officer, National Oilwell Varco

---

National Oilwell Varco (NOV) is a manufacturer of oil well equipment, such as drill heads. This is a story of how NOV took a pragmatic approach to the cloud when they needed to get rid of legacy technical debt. Their goals: more capabilities and lower costs. Cloud transformation helped NOV power quantum changes in their IT infrastructure, even during challenging economic times while still delivering. Alex Philips is the Chief Information Officer at NOV. In this next journey, he shares how his team found a way for their globally distributed organization to be secure while upgrading the tools and processes they used in the cloud.

I was CISO of National Oilwell Varco (NOV) when the bottom dropped out of the oil and gas market. Spot prices for crude plummeted below $30 per barrel. I had a long career at NOV, working my way up from system administrator. Over that time I had established trust with the executive leadership and my teams. I had 20 people in my security team with plans and budgets to grow that to 40. Shortly after the crisis hit, our CIO departed and I stepped into the dual role of CIO and CISO. My primary task? Cut costs. Do more with less.

The downturn impacted the entire oil and gas exploration industry, including our customers. Once profitable at $70 per barrel, everyone needed to cut costs to face a new reality. Part of the response was the digitization of oil and gas exploration. The mantra was "more data." We began to instrument our products. We could save on wear and tear and replacement costs for our customers. Of course, they were making decisions—using data—that allowed them to make better choices about where and when to drill. Over time, the industry has achieved profitability at $40 per barrel.

NOV Footprint

As a company, we had beefed up our IT security in the 2010 to 2014 timeframe. It was time to think about a refresh cycle, but many of our larger locations were upgrading from 1-gigabit to 10-gigabit networks. There is a huge cost difference in security appliances to make that transition and to handle 10-gigabits of traffic. We were looking at a $2 million investment just to maintain the same capability. And what about the OPEX to maintain all that gear? How could we reduce that?

It started with Office 365

I remember everyone was talking about the cloud. Microsoft was pushing really hard on Office 365. We had almost a hundred Microsoft Exchange servers globally to maintain that contained over a petabyte of email storage. It was going to cost $12 million to continue down that path of managing our own email, and it was only growing larger. I remember deciding, "Let's just give our email to Microsoft to manage."

So we began that journey, a change to the way we did business in IT. Before the downturn, we had purchased all of our own servers and did everything in-house. The downturn got us thinking and led to a strategic pivot towards the cloud.

"An interesting fallout from this transformation to the cloud is that we actually expanded our technology footprint."

I remember thinking, "All these security appliances, this is ridiculous." All of those mobile employees did not work behind those security appliances. They were going directly to the internet. With the Zscaler cloud service, we could protect them no matter where they were.

We did not have a sanctioned cloud storage solution at that time. However, the move to Office 365 gave every user a terabyte of storage on Microsoft OneDrive. Now, they can share data and folders with third parties and be more effective.

An interesting fallout from this transformation to the cloud is that we actually expanded our technology footprint. Ironically, shifting to Microsoft cloud services with secure access from anywhere meant we could also support iPads, Macs, and even iOS phones.

The reaction from our employees was amusing. Here we were slashing tens of millions of dollars from our budget, while at the same time enabling modern tools. Our users were thinking IT was spending so much on all this new stuff, when in reality we were spending dramatically less and delivering more.

Embracing SaaS applications

It's funny how cloud adoption happens. Often it is organic. Users use new technology before IT gets dragged in. Smartsheet for project tracking and collaboration is an example. Users had flocked to Smartsheet, and the IT group got pulled in to manage identities and access. We have adopted it as a sanctioned application.

We transitioned our limited unsanctioned Dropbox users to OneDrive. We have also seen a massive uptick in Slack usage for collaboration. IT has not embraced it, but thanks to our cloud security service, we are comfortable with people using it even though it is not yet officially sanctioned. We definitely see the shift to cloud applications. We have even begun the journey of moving HR and corporate finance to the cloud.

Shifting our HR and corporate finance to the cloud is a major leap for us. These applications are publicly available over the internet instead of in our data centers. I don't have direct access to the underlying database, and I don't need to maintain it. Everything is done through APIs that I don't even have to schedule outages and deployments for upgrades.

"It's funny how cloud adoption happens. Often it is organic. Users use new technology before IT gets dragged in."

A multi-cloud strategy

We are taking a pragmatic approach to the cloud. We don't have a cloud-first strategy; we have a "cloud when it makes sense" strategy. We need to get rid of legacy technical debt. It needs to be cheaper, and it needs to give us more capability.

And then there are our internal applications. We count over 2,000 official internal applications, and I am sure there are more we don't know about. We have rarely forced people to quit using an application. At one point we had 70 different ERP systems. It costs millions to change ERPs and is very disruptive. We have learned to live this way and perform lots of consolidation of financials to do the mapping of general ledgers and reporting. We also have a data warehouse that allows everyone to use their existing ERP, while we can see the whole picture.

For public cloud we have adopted a multi-cloud strategy. We do have IaaS on Amazon and Azure and are actively looking at adding Google and Oracle. We are only moving workloads to the cloud where it makes sense. We have started a project to do a full analysis to figure out what it truly costs to host a server in our data centers.

Given that, we are not looking at re-doing most of our applications. When the next cycle of higher oil prices comes, the questions will be, "How do we refactor the business? How do we look at machine learning? How do we look at containerization?" We are at that beginning phase where we are deciding to not make a monolithic big app but rather 20 to 30 micro services that can be tied together, something that is cloud ready.

The cloud delivers more functionality and at a lower cost

Take Zscaler as an example of "just software." We were able to get rid of our expensive and hard-to-maintain security appliances, while taking advantage of the scale and redundancy of Zscaler. We now point our traffic to two different Zscaler data centers. I did not have the money to do this in the old appliance world as it would have cost twice as much. We get more features, cheaper, along with more capability.

Office 365 is the same way. More features, lower cost, more capability like OneDrive and Teams. We are confident that moving HR and corporate finance to the cloud will have the same advantages.

> "We were able to get rid of our expensive and hard-to-maintain security appliances."

Leveling the playing field with cloud

IT has always been a competitive advantage. It drives the dual objectives of serving more customers and reducing costs.

But now the cloud is leveling the playing field. I worry about how cloud transformation is going to change the competitive landscape in our industry. In the old days, if you were a small "mom and pop," you did not have data analytics, massive data warehouses, or a digitally collaborative platform. That was reserved for large organizations such as ours with over 20 years of investments in systems, processes, and people. All of a sudden, the small shops can get better IT in the cloud. They don't have to hire IT people, buy and deploy servers, or build data centers. They can essentially leapfrog us without making a huge investment. To their customers, they have better technology than the large players.

Network transformation with SD-WAN and cloud security

We had eleven internet egress points around the world optimally arranged in the traditional MPLS hub-and-spoke architecture.

Currently, we are on a journey to more of a mesh with SD-WAN. Our network team is excited by the promise of SD-WAN: use software to control the network and deploy low-cost boxes across the network. This gives us internet circuits that are ten times faster than traditional MPLS dedicated circuits, without any impact on quality. With the SD-WAN approach, the data in transit is always encrypted, addressing potential issues we may encounter in many of the countries where we operate.

"Our mantra: You should be able to access your data anytime from anywhere on any device (within reason)."

Our MPLS mandate was that the network had to be reliable, always up. We think with SD-WAN we can failover to cellular or our employees can head to a Starbucks to get access. Considering the fact that our MPLS budget has exceeded $400K per month just to service the 100 United States facilities, there are a lot of financial benefits to be clawed back by moving to SD-WAN, where we point all internet traffic to Zscaler's cloud security platform. We are also excited about the cost saving potential of applying this to our other

500 global facilities. Of our internet traffic, 20% is Office 365. Another big chunk is YouTube, which we used to block but now allow because users were watching so many work-related instructional videos.

Local internet connections through an aggregator

We had hoped that we could find ISPs for each location, even assumed that a facility manager—who already was responsible for power, water, light, heating, and physical security—would be able to find good internet providers. This was a bit too optimistic and not moving as fast as we hoped, so we found a broker to manage all those connections. It cost a little more, but our management requirements are much lower.

Enhanced security

On the endpoint, we transitioned to whitelisting several years ago. We tried multiple traditional antivirus companies, but they just couldn't keep up with the threats. We used to have 100 machines a month that had to be quarantined and re-imaged. Now with cloud security and whitelisting, it is one a month. We don't have a malware or ransomware problem at all.

The number one attack vector is email, so we invested in advanced sandbox solutions for attachments and URL rewrites for links.

Getting executive buy-in for transformation takes work

On the matter of getting buy-in, I am a little bit spoiled. I have been with the company for twenty years, from executive support for PCs to servers, ERP, networks, and architecture. At some point along the way, I led our teams that designed or built most of our infrastructure. As we acquired hundreds of companies, I led the teams to integrate them into our collective whole. I have gained a lot of trust as a problem solver. This is why after we experienced a security incident, they turned to me to build a security team. When it came time to replace the CIO, they turned to me again. You have to establish that level of trust. Deliver on what you say you are going to do and the executive team will trust your direction.

The biggest challenge for me has not been executive buy-in, but it's getting buy-in from my IT staff. When I put these big audacious goals out there, when I said get rid of appliances and move to Zscaler, I got push back. We had a 90-day deployment proposal from Zscaler. I told my staff they had 60 days and they got it done.

Advice to CxOs—What to do

You have to have pervasive visibility. If you don't, there is no way to know what is going on your endpoints. Most endpoints are not in your walled garden anymore. Can you even tell if you have a problem?

You need to look at this as a win-win situation. I think we will all end up with a hybrid strategy. Use cloud where it makes sense. That will be different for every company. I can't see a reason to be locked into any single cloud provider of IaaS.

IT leaders need to understand that the days of simply having IT as a competitive advantage are over. IT is just turning into a cost to do business. Even the guy that digs a ditch has a website and email. You have to figure out how to tie everything together to create greater insights on your business to get back the competitive advantage.

Advice to CxOs—What not to do

I would avoid sticking to the same vendors that you have always used, as their main goal is to preserve or grow revenue, not save you money. Look at all the upstarts. A smaller company can offer amazing technology and support and is not stuck in the old mindset.

Avoid complacency. If something is not working, you have to change. If you committed to something and realize it was a mistake, suck it up and move on. It feels like we had our heads in the sand during the boom times. The oil crash forced us to look at everything and transform how we do business. We experienced a forced wake-up call and we recognize that we still have a long journey ahead of us.

Chapter 5 Takeaways

Office 365 is driving the transition to the cloud for many organizations. While cost reductions and productivity gains may be the result, the business must be cloud-ready before embarking on an Office 365 migration project. Be aware that network bandwidth will skyrocket when you move to Office 365. Ensure that your users can get to Office 365 as directly as possible from each location. This invariably means that local internet breakouts will be needed.

- Pay for local internet breakout with savings from reduced MPLS circuits.

- Look for ways to reduce the number of hops between a user and Microsoft's data centers.

- Additionally, mobile users will need to get access from wherever they are.

- Use bandwidth throttling to balance Office 365 bandwidth consumption against other critical apps.

- Don't make the mistake of hosting DNS in the data center.

CHAPTER 6

A Reference Architecture for Secure Cloud Transformation

———————————————⌄A⌄———————————————

*"This ideal reference architecture can be defined simply:
A cloud layer that connects all users to all applications,
based on business policy, with a consistent end-user experience, no matter where users are or what device they are
using—all at lower cost, while being simple to manage."*

Darryl Staskowski, Senior Vice President and Chief Information Officer, Kelly Services

———————————————⌄———————————————

Legacy network and security models worked historically because applications and users were all on the corporate network. The internet was just another network that happened to contain new threats, so security appliances were deployed to protect the network from the wild west that was the internet.

That all changed as users left the corporate network to become the highly dispersed and mobile workforce of today. At the same time, the application landscape has evolved dramatically with the migration to the cloud, where they can be supported with high availability, low latency access, and elastic computing to accommodate varying demands. This invariably shifts the center of gravity away from the corporate network and data center, making the internet the new corporate network.

A reference architecture presents an ideal: the form of a perfectly envisioned and executed solution. In the following section of this chapter we will outline some common architectural phases many of the leading IT organizations interviewed in the book went through during their transformation journey.

Architectural Phases for Secure Cloud Transformation

Stage 1: Pre-transformation

As we've covered in this book so far, the traditional corporate network architecture has not evolved in over two to three decades. The network topology is basically spoke sites connected to regionally or centralized hub sites over MPLS or IPSec VPNs.

The network supports internet traffic by deploying stacks of security appliances to be able to apply policy for traffic that is egressing the perimeter while allowing inbound access from outside the network. Often, this access mechanism is accomplished on a regional basis where there are limited sites around the world. However, it starts to become cost prohibitive to support and scale these full stacks of appliances at every site where you are required to provide internet access.

In this stage, all your users and applications are on-premises, and they connect back to the network via a VPN. Also, the internet access they often require is not business critical, as illustrated in Figure 6.1.

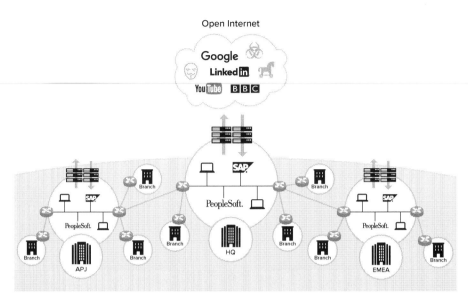

Figure 6.1 Stage 1: Pre-transformed state

The architecture for legacy IT at this stage is also known as a data center-centric architecture and is summarized in Table 6.1 below.

Legacy IT

Architecture	Data center-centric
Applications	Reside in the data center
Users	On your network — either in the office or remotely conneced via VPN
	Limited use of 4G/wireless; largely connected to the data center
Network	Trusted network — a private network that you can control or manage that connects branches to regional hub sites over MPLS or IPSec VPNs
	Hub-and-spoke
	To access internal, internet, or SaaS applications, user must be on the corporate network
Security	Will need to secure the network to protect users and applications
	Build a perimeter or moat with firewalls and proxies
	Security is tied to the network

Table 6.1 Data center-centric architecture

Stage 2: Hybrid IT

The second stage typically depicts a hybrid environment. In this scenario:

- Some of your applications have moved to the cloud, either as SaaS applications, e.g., Office 365 or as IaaS running on Microsoft Azure, AWS or Google Cloud. Other applications are still on premises.

- Your users are mobile and can operate outside your previously well-defined corporate perimeter. They're no longer working just within the confines of the corporate office; they are outside and are accessing those cloud applications directly.

- As more and more business-critical applications move to the cloud you are now operating in a world where your center of gravity is shifting up to the cloud.

Through network transformation at this hybrid stage as shown in Figure 6.2, you will typically route your internet-bound traffic to the internet or the cloud over local internet connections, and route corporate traffic to your data center over the traditional MPLS network.

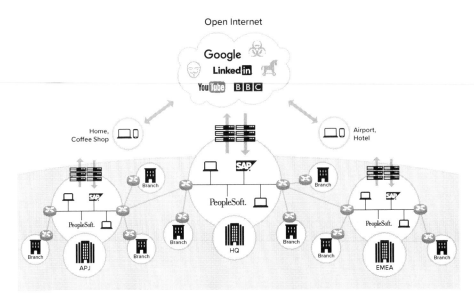

Figure 6.2 Stage 2: Hybrid IT

The attributes for this Hybrid IT stage is summarized in Table 6.2 below:

Hybrid IT

Architecture	Data center and cloud-centric
Applications	Most of the applications are in the data center, and there are an increasing number SaaS and cloud-based applications being accessed
Users	Users are mostly on the network. To access the internet or cloud-based applications, users do not need to connect to the network, and can connect directly
Network	Both trusted and untrusted networks (internet)
	Hybrid — hub-and-spoke as well as direct-to-cloud
	To access internal applications, users must connect to the network. For SaaS and internet applications, user go directly over the internet and do not connect to the network
Security	The private network is secured and cloud security is enabled for access to the internet and for SaaS applications
	The perimeter is limited to data centers where the internal applications reside
	Some security is still tied to the network

Table 6.2 Hybrid IT architecture

Stage 3: Direct-to-cloud

This stage depicts the final stage in the evolution of your infrastructure, whereby your organization has acknowledged that your center of gravity is moving to the internet and that the internet is becoming your new corporate network. Your users are no longer within the well-defined corporate network, and your applications are no longer there either. In this stage, not only does the user's internet and SaaS traffic go over the internet, but the traffic for internal applications that are hosted in either the data center or the public cloud such as Azure or AWS, also goes over the internet. The public cloud or data center are both treated as destinations for these applications as shown in Figure 6.3.

In essence, by leveraging the internet as the new corporate network, embracing a cloud security architecture, and surrounding it with a set of best-of-breed services, your secure cloud transformation journey is complete.

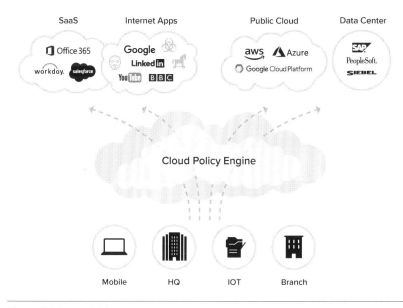

Figure 6.3 Stage 3: Direct-to-cloud state

Table 6.3 below summarizes the attributes of a cloud-centric architecture:

Direct-to-Cloud

Architecture	Cloud-centric
Applications	Most applications are either SaaS or in the public cloud, with some still in the data center
Users	A large number of users are not on the network. Users directly connect to the internet or to internal applications over any network including 4G/5G, even while in the office
Network	Mostly untrusted neworks — the internet becomes the corporate WAN
	Direct-to-cloud
	To access internal or external applications, users do not connect to the network. They simply connect to applications over any network
Security	Network security no longer works — you cannot control a network that you cannot secure
	Securely connect users to applications
	Security is decoupled from the network, and the network becomes just a form of transport

Table 6.3 Cloud-centric architecture

Kelly Services

A Blueprint for Secure Cloud Transformation

Company:	Kelly Services	Revenue:	$5.5 billion
Sector:	Workforce Augmentation	Employees:	10,000
Driver:	Darryl Staskowski	Countries:	22
Role:	SVP & CIO	Locations:	870

Company IT Footprint: In 2010, when Kelly Services first started their transformation journey, they were supporting over 10,000 employees across 870 locations in 22 countries. This infrastructure was supported by 17 different MPLS network providers. By the time they completed Phase 1 of their transformation journey, they had reduced their MPLS footprint from 870 locations to 30 with the help of SD-WAN services.

"The cloud transformation journey is to a simpler, more effective, more resilient IT infrastructure. Taking a phased approach will reduce disruption to operations, while generating the cost savings that can fuel each new phase."

Darryl Staskowski,
Senior Vice President and Chief Information Officer, Kelly Services

---

Darryl Staskowski is the SVP and CIO at Kelly Services, one of the largest workforce augmentation companies in the world. The company has followed a strategy of growth through acquisitions in countries in the major regions, which led to a globally disparate set of networks and applications. Kelly Services went through a five-phase cloud transformation journey. Darryl shares his experiences next on how cloud transformation helped his organization deliver solutions that created a better user experience and enhanced business agility.

In the words of Darryl Staskowski:

The pre-transformation state

In 2010, we had 870 locations in 22 countries supported by 17 different MPLS network providers at Kelly. With data centers in three major regions and separate disaster recovery data centers for backup, our architecture had grown into one which is similar to many large organizations today.

Each data center was protected by a different set of legacy appliances. They had next-gen firewalls from three different vendors and proxy devices, all managed by separate regional teams aligned with each business unit.

Business needs drive transformation

But architectures don't drive change, business needs do. And in our case, it was the lack of consistent collaboration tools among the divisions and regions that brought home the realization that change was required. We wanted our executives and teams around the globe to be able to use the same tools for collaboration, video, and document sharing, and have the same experience when it comes to availability and performance, no matter where they were.

Our IT teams were so busy addressing issues with so many different systems that new IT projects, such as rolling out Wi-Fi to each office and deploying common collaboration tools, were not getting done.

On top of that, the overall posture of the organization was in an unknowable state. All those networks were difficult to manage. There was no way to ensure that security policies were constantly enforced across all these devices. We were starting to be faced with significant capital expenditures and continued operational expenditures just to keep doing business as usual if we didn't make a change.

The Five Phases of Our Transformation Journey

We knew that cloud transformation would deliver solutions that helped create a better experience for our users, help us reduce business risk while enhancing our business agility, and provide us a competitive advantage, all while reducing our total cost of ownership (TCO).

Our ideal reference architecture could simply be defined as a cloud layer that connects all users to all applications, based on business policy, with a consistent end-user experience, no matter where users are or what device they are using—all at lower cost, while being simple to manage.

"Our transformation journey followed five phases, which started with a focus on a network purpose-built for leveraging the SaaS applications."

This is all that our internal architects needed to start our cloud transformation. The process for us at Kelly Services started with applications moving to the cloud. Our transformation journey followed five phases, which started with a focus on a network purpose-built for leveraging the SaaS applications the business demanded, while creating an enhanced infrastructure posture at a lower TCO. Once the branch network was complete, the focus shifted to moving data center workloads to IaaS and delivering a consistent end-user experience for access to all business systems, regardless of where they were hosted.

Phase 1. Migration to Office 365

The first step for us was to standardize on a single email and business productivity suite. We chose Microsoft's Business Productivity Online Suite (BPOS). BPOS was an early version of Microsoft Office 365. Moving the entire organization to Office 365 accomplished much of the collaboration experience that we needed with SharePoint, and the rest of the suite adding to their capabilities.

We also moved to a standard firewall platform in each of our global data centers managed by a single MSSP. We deployed 24 additional firewalls to sites with more than 80 people, so we could achieve local breakouts for internet access.

In this phase, we also consolidated carriers by awarding a single contract for global network services. This consolidation reduced the MPLS footprint from 870 locations to 30 with the help of SD-WAN services, where most office traffic was delivered to an MPLS backbone via an IPsec tunnel over the internet.

The next step was to eliminate utility services in each office. DNS and Active Directory Domain Controllers were consolidated into data centers.

Print and file servers were also moved. Now, the IT services in the remote offices were simplified. Just end-user devices and LANs had to be managed.

The end state after Phase 1:

- Nine data centers with MPLS-only connectivity. All internet traffic from branch offices backhauled to the data centers before being routed to the internet.

- 24 locations with MPLS circuits and internet protected by UTM security appliances managed by a single service provider.

- There were 870 small offices with local internet connections and perimeter devices to terminate IPsec tunnels into the MPLS backbone. Note that the internet was used as transport, but local breakouts were not enabled. Traffic to the SaaS applications still went to the MPLS backbone first, where it then went through the regional data centers.

- Consolidated utility computing (DNS, file, and print servers) to data centers.

These changes created cost savings that funded the remaining phases of our transformation. The networking changes alone saved 60% from our budget for MPLS circuits. It also created a better internet experience for those in the regional and country headquarters, where UTM appliances were deployed. Our IT operations were vastly simplified with common email, SharePoint, and a single MPLS and SD-WAN provider.

Phase 2. Local breakouts for web traffic at all locations

In the next phase, we embarked on a project to introduce local internet breakouts to 870 small offices, so we could take advantage of Skype and SharePoint Online and any SaaS application or online resource.

This was done using the Zscaler cloud security service for web traffic for ports 80 and 443. PAC files were pushed to personal computers that were deployed in each office. Zscaler maintained a global PAC file that used geolocation to determine which Zscaler global data center was the most appropriate for security and policy enforcement.

Providing connections to Office 365 is challenging for any organization. More than 700 separate rules were required, because the branch devices did not support domain name rules, and applications like Skype require more than just ports 80/443. Every time Microsoft provisioned new IP address ranges for its services, the SD-WAN device configuration needed to be updated.

Phase 3. Local Breakout of all internet traffic

The next phase we embarked on was to build full VPN IPsec tunnels from each branch office to the Zscaler cloud for all internet bound traffic. Zscaler essentially became the default route to the internet. Our network service provider provisioned very simple routers at each of our offices that could send internet traffic to the nearest Zscaler data center and internal traffic to our corporate data centers through tunnels that reached the MPLS back-bone. The branch router or SD-WAN device were very simple to manage as there were no complicated rule sets to be enforced.

Now, all traffic over all ports and protocols was being routed to Zscaler, taking advantage of its full Cloud Firewall capability. Instead of the more than 700 policies that were required, all our offices had a common set of only 12 policies.

At the same time, the requirement for managing the firewalls at our larger offices was reduced considerably, thanks to the Cloud Firewall service.

Application prioritization for Office 365 traffic

Office 365 posed a bandwidth problem for us at Kelly. It was a critical application, so it needed guaranteed performance and responsiveness, but at the same time, because OneDrive started to replace the local file servers, file transfers could bog everything down. By implementing bandwidth controls available within Zscaler, Office 365 could be guaranteed 30% of all bandwidth, but also be limited to no more than 50%, so that other apps continued to work effectively.

"End users should not be the ones making decisions about how they connect to IT resources."

A lesson learned during this phase was that end users should not be the ones making decisions about how they connect to IT resources. Many were still launching their VPN client when they were connecting to Office 365 applications, leading to performance issues. The choice of connectivity should be solved by technology, not the end user.

This phase delivered a consistent end-user experience across our entire network no matter where our users were located. It simplified our overall architecture dramatically, as every user was protected all the time.

Phase 4. Internal application migration to the public cloud

Once our network configuration was architected to provide consistent, secure access to applications, the next phase could begin—migration of our applications to the cloud to improve delivery and resiliency. By moving customer-facing applications to Azure or AWS, we could begin to consolidate our data centers, while improving the experience of mobile workers.

Tight integration between Office 365 and Azure

A bake-off was performed between AWS and Azure. Our team initially picked AWS, because there was a more mature marketplace of options to select from like virtual load balancers and firewalls, but it was Azure's tight integration with Microsoft and Office 365 that was the deciding factor. We moved customer-facing applications to Azure, with the goal of making them available to our end users without requiring the use of legacy VPN clients.

Attempt to securely access public cloud applications with virtualized security appliances

To protect our applications, we made an attempt to build the same sort of legacy infrastructure that had existed in our data center. Virtualized instances of load balancers and next-gen firewall appliances were deployed in front of the applications. This setup became prohibitively expensive, as scaling these solutions to support more applications in the future required more and more licenses. It was unsustainable and became hard to justify a business case that actually made it more expensive to host applications in the cloud than in legacy on-premise data centers.

We consolidated four of our data centers in the Asia-Pacific region to one, which reduced the number of sites managed by the third-party MSSP.

CIO Journey | Kelly Services

Meanwhile, our North American data centers were soon to be migrated to state-of-the-art third-party hosting environments.

Phase 5. Secure and fast access to internal applications

We kicked off a *Kelly Anywhere* mobile workforce program, and volunteers were moved away from legacy desktop collaboration spaces to next-generation collaboration spaces hosted in cloud environments. The project was deemed a success, because it provided a consistent user experience for application access, both inside and outside offices.

In this final phase of cloud transformation, we are developing a long-term plan to leverage software defined perimeter (SDP) principles to deliver a consistent end-user experience, regardless of where the application is hosted or where the user is located. Investments in technology are being made to enable future mobile workforce programs, M&A consolidation projects, and as a reference architecture for a future zero-trust network model.

We made a critical decision not to deploy legacy remote access solutions in the new data center. Instead, Zscaler Private Access (ZPA) is being deployed. This cloud-built application access layer integrates with Active Directory and connects authorized users to their applications with no additional hardware or technology in the data center or in front of the applications in Azure.

We leveraged the SDP solution as a new playbook for mergers and acquisitions. The business side has stressed that fast onboarding of new employees after an acquisition was critical, as well as the quick spin off in a sale. Instead of focusing on integrating two networks, it was decided that ZPA would be rolled out to provide access to required applications for future M&A activities. Policies that only allow specific users to access specific applications can be quickly deployed.

A transition plan was established to move the network to a zero-trust stance long term. Only users coming from the SDP would be granted access to the data centers. The plan was worked into the continuing operations plan by scheduling switch-overs as offices moved their locations (as they did on average every three years) or when internet connections needed to be upgraded.

The move to SDP would free up IT resources that had been focused on the day-to-day challenge of securing 900 branches. In the future, we will be able to focus on improvements in the data center and IaaS platforms. The vastly simplified access control lists (ACLs) in the data center just have to provide for SDP connections.

The results of a phased approach

Our cloud transformation journey is to a simpler, more effective, more resilient IT infrastructure. Taking a phased approach will reduce disruption to operations, while generating the cost savings that can fuel each new phase.

The new perimeter is identity. The location of the users and the applications they need is no longer a concern. A focus on identity and protecting the data center is more cost effective and a better use of resources.

"The new perimeter is identity."

Transformation timeline

The total time frame for network transformation is dependent on a number of variables. For instance, an organization with 60 locations all on one service provider could move to a cloud-enabled network architecture in four to six months. An organization with 900 locations and multiple service providers could take between 12-18 months.

Other variables include:

- Contractual terms of current providers. Companies using multiple providers globally may wait to move to new architectures as their current contracts expire to avoid significant penalties.

- Is it a project or a program? You will want to have seasoned project managers that can communicate the status of the project to both internal IT and business stakeholders. Communicate the value of the project with the business—don't just treat the project like a standard upgrade where you do it during a maintenance window during a holiday or weekend and not tell anyone.

- Size of team working on deployment. Most organizations will not have a dedicated team to deploy the new architecture and it will fall either on the Network Operations or Network Engineering teams that are also responsible for other tasks. If that is the case, start with deploying new architecture and configurations as you have to touch each location (example, when a branch office moves). Then implement a process to move a small number per week on top of daily operational duties and start to increase that number as the various teams become more comfortable with the work.

- What applications are moving to the cloud? Are they just email, legacy business systems, Salesforce? In some cases, the migration of business systems or adoption of new cloud-based tools will drive business process changes. The deployments can be dictated by the pace at which the business processes change to leverage the new tools.

Lessons learned: what worked well and what didn't

1. Leverage an ISP aggregator.

- Find a company that can deliver and manage local broadband internet connections at your locations. You want to leverage local providers as you will get the most bandwidth for the cheapest cost.

- You don't want to have to manage dozens of internet providers. Find one that you give a street address of your location to and they provide the options.

- Ideally you will want more than one internet connection from different providers at your critical locations for redundancy.

- Buying internet from the large service providers globally will be almost as expensive as the legacy MPLS networks.

2. Include all disciplines of IT in the program kickoff.

The new direct-to-internet architecture will touch network, security, endpoint, server, and application teams. Include each team from the beginning with a clear end-state goal. This will help alleviate the political problems that pop up in transformation programs when the goals of each IT discipline are not communicated across the various leadership team. Everyone has to understand "what is in it for me."

3. Build a reinvestment model with finance.

- Organizations will most likely recognize savings as they start to move to a cloud-enabled network architecture and move their data center workloads. Build a model with finance teams to reinvest a portion of the savings into technology that focuses on improving end-user experience.

- Find technology solutions that can monitor the experience of end users regardless of where they are located and send alerts when specific thresholds are met. This allows IT to focus on building proactive support processes as opposed to waiting for end users to complain about performance issues.

Successful transformation is often led by senior IT leaders

Leadership should empower employees to take risks and encourage them to challenge the status quo. Look at network, security, application, and identity architectures differently. CxOs need to convey their goals in terms of end-user experience, SaaS/IaaS adoption, enhanced security, and cost savings to all of IT. IT teams need to understand the overall context of the architecture they are tasked with building, as just replacing legacy point products will no longer work towards the goals of the CxOs.

CxOs must build the case for transformation with their business stakeholders on improved end-user experience (consistent access to applications regardless of location, which can in turn drive mobile workforce programs), enhanced security (the threats are not going away, they are multiplying), and cost savings (most organizations are not "IT-focused" and their efforts should be focused on supporting their business, not managing email servers).

Multiple disciplines of IT with a collective mindset for change

The transformation programs will cover all of IT. CxOs need to sponsor the programs and make sure representation from each group participates in steering committees.

Overcome the political challenges associated with changing legacy architectures that have worked for 30+ years. The new architectures that support a cloud-enabled enterprise are very foreign to people who have been supporting legacy network, security, data center, and application infrastructure. CxOs need to focus on the paradigm shift of service ownership. The capabilities to support this architecture will no longer be delivered by point products sitting in a data center managed locally, but the skill set from the teams will still be required. CxOs will still need people with network, security, and application skill sets in the cloud-first world, in addition to a progressive mindset. Their teams will have to learn that they deliver the capabilities to their business stakeholders in a different way.

Chapter 6 Takeaways

Some of the enterprise IT leaders in this book have highlighted that they have typically followed these three phases during their transformation journey. Some IT leaders have also created steps within phases two and three of more bite-sized chunks for their organizations to consume. Doing it this way helped them transform in smaller stages—for example, they did not have to move all their applications to SaaS and PaaS applications in one hit. Nor did they have to fork-lift their on-premises security stack out of the gate. Some leaders preferred to transform critical pieces of their functionality first, and then chose to deploy additional capabilities over time.

One major airline carrier chose to embark upon their transformation journey in one hit—they forklifted their web proxy out and deployed a cloud security architecture in production in a weekend, with 80,000 users going live. A leading global bank chose to deploy a cloud security architecture on top of their current on-premises security stack to enable SSL encryption. They left everything they had initially in place with an additive layer of security in the cloud. Other major organizations such as GE, have focused on completely transforming their IT infrastructure and practices, and invested three years in executing on their complex global network transformation project.

Whatever your chosen set of steps and phases for cloud transformation may be, clearly define your business and technical goals and outline a plan and a reference architecture that best suits these desired outcomes for success. Be sure to draw from the many real-world testimonials and insights from this book in helping you navigate that journey.

CHAPTER 7

Perspectives of Leading Cloud Providers

———————————⋀———————————

"The key is to just get started. Five years ago, cloud was still relatively new for a lot of enterprises but we're now entering an adoption phase where the majority of new systems are now cloud-based. Cloud has reached the mainstream and moving down that path is the right approach."

Scott Guthrie, Executive Vice President, Microsoft

———————————⋁———————————

Cloud computing abstraction levels

It's important to understand the different abstraction levels in cloud computing. From there, the challenges of "refactoring" applications for the cloud can be addressed.

The concept of SaaS is easy to grasp: basically, an application reached through a web browser. But what about IaaS and PaaS? One simple way to think about these is:

- IaaS: Host
- PaaS: Build
- SaaS: Consume

IaaS is the compute platform. The service, be it Amazon Web Services (AWS), Microsoft Azure, or Google Cloud Platform, provides virtualization, the servers, storage, and networking. You can think of IaaS as an extension of your data center without any requirement to purchase hardware. You do not have to configure machines, connect them to your Network Attached Storage (NAS), or manage the switches and routers to reach it.

PaaS goes several steps further. Now the service also provides and maintains the operating system (OS), middleware, and runtime environment. You only have to worry about your application and its configuration. Microsoft's Azure Cloud Services are PaaS offerings. They spin up web roles and worker roles. The web role is the web server (IIS) and everything needed to support it: a virtualized instance of Windows Server and all the connectors. The worker roles are set up to run particular operations such as taking user input and processing it. The only things you are responsible for with PaaS are the application itself and the data.

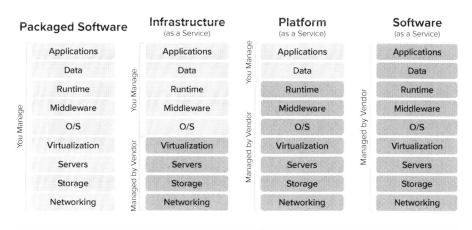

Figure 7.1 From packaged software to as-a-service; Credit: Albert Barron

The ultimate level of cloud service, in terms of the spectrum of responsibility for the components, is SaaS, where the entire stack is maintained by the service provider, such as Salesforce.

Cloud Service Providers

It is no surprise that cloud services are dominated by Amazon, Microsoft, and Google. Each company continues to develop extensive infrastructure to host its own services and came to the realization that the systems they built could be decoupled from their primary businesses and offered up as an easy-to-consume service. This chapter highlights first-hand perspectives of the leading cloud service providers as they have continued to evolve their platforms and services.

How Microsoft is Accelerating Enterprise Cloud Adoption

Scott Guthrie, Executive Vice President, Microsoft

───────────◇───────────

"There is enormous growth across our cloud products. This includes Azure, Office 365, and Dynamics 365. Azure has nearly doubled every year and Dynamics 365 revenue has grown greater than 60% since we began disclosing it in the third quarter of fiscal year 2017."

Scott Guthrie, Executive Vice President, Microsoft

───────────◇───────────

Microsoft came to the cloud through scaling its search engine. Bing was meant to compete with Google Search and required a scalable infrastructure on which to build. Satya Nadella, now Microsoft's CEO, launched Bing in 2009. In his book *Hit Refresh*, Nadella says Bing helped jump-start Microsoft's journey to the cloud. When he took over the Servers and Tools Business (STB) at Microsoft he sensed the cloud would be, in his words, "the biggest transformation of Microsoft in a generation."

Scott Guthrie shares Microsoft's journey to the cloud, in addition to having one of the fastest growing SaaS solutions on the planet, Office 365, which is driving cloud adoption in the enterprise.

Microsoft started its cloud journey nearly 15 years ago, when Ray Ozzie was one of the key people advocating for the cloud. At that time, we had two teams driving our cloud journey: The Office team and our Business Productivity Online Standard (BPOS) initiative.

Things really accelerated around 2010 and in the last eight years we have brought together the Microsoft Cloud, which includes platforms and services such as Azure, Office 365, and Dynamics 365. Today, we're thinking about the migration to the cloud in terms of productivity, and how the overall technology needs of SaaS, PaaS, and infrastructure bind together to deliver business solutions.

Like many other enterprises whose legacy extends far beyond the cloud era, cloud transformation is a journey that we're still on, and one we hope to continue indefinitely. Thankfully, it's one with which we're seeing tremendous customer success, which leads to success from a business perspective as well.

Classic dilemma

A decade ago, if you asked whether customers would rather have control or technology transition, they would choose control. This is a classic enterprise dilemma, but I would say a transition is too important. One of the problems leaders of enterprise companies historically have is not asking for transition like from command line to GUI. The future is going to happen, whether they are convinced or not, and in that case, you must act even though your best customers are saying they're not sure that's what they want.

If you don't transition, by the time customer demand develops, it's too late. Sometimes, if you act incorrectly, they never come—and in that case, you will also go out of business. Technology is a tricky thing; it's not just cloud specific. For all technology transitions, timing is difficult. Companies have to have the fortitude to move even before there is a strong customer demand. In our case, we made the call in 2010 to transition in earnest to the cloud. We leaned into the cloud before there even was customer signal or demand. That meant that when the market really started shifting a couple of years ago we had already built out the infrastructure, data centers, and productivity software in the cloud-based environment. We were ready to ride that wave.

"If you don't transition, by the time customer demand develops, it's too late."

We've worked to secure a strong position in the market in terms of both having the enterprise credibility, but more importantly, having the enterprise credibility in the cloud space. We have a cloud portfolio that isn't just on the shelf and ready, but is integrated well. This is not a space where we are just doing lots of acquisitions, which leads to a very disjointed product set. While we do acquisitions, a lot of the cloud infrastructure and software that we have has been built up more organically and composes very well as a result. It is integrated in ways that provide differentiation that ultimately enables customers to be successful.

At Microsoft, we eat our own dog food

We are one of the biggest enterprise consumers of the cloud. Some of our customers have 400,000 employees that are using us, while we only have 130,000 employees. So, there are probably bigger companies now that use the cloud just because they are bigger in terms of employees. About 90% of our IT systems now run in Azure and in Office 365 and Dynamics 365. We drive a tremendous amount of consumption and with the savings we've been able to redeploy resources to other strategic investments.

We have always had this philosophy at Microsoft called "eat our own dog food," which is: how do we run our own business on the software that we sell to end customers? Our email is all hosted in Office 365. Our SharePoint sites are in Office 365. Our SAP systems now run inside Azure. We do quarter end close in the cloud. We have one of the largest ERP backends in the world. All these complicated components run inside Azure, within our infrastructure. This includes our identity systems, management security systems, build systems, and dev-tech systems.

In addition, since we "eat our own dog food," we harden our systems every time we talk to a customer. For example, if we are walking a customer through SAP migration, we are simultaneously walking through our own SAP migration. We can share our own experiences with migration, and the customers are therefore able to understand all the details in a large-scale infrastructure migration, from the perspective of our own IT team.

Our cloud is growing fast

There is enormous growth across our cloud products. This includes Azure, Office 365 and Dynamics 365. Azure has nearly doubled every year and

Dynamics 365 revenue has grown greater than 60% since we began disclosing it in the third quarter of fiscal year 2017. The combination of our products helps employees be more productive, connect with customers, run their operations, and use data intelligence better than ever before.

I think one of the reasons why our SaaS software has grown so fast is that, historically, deploying those types of large solutions on premises took time. Previously it would have taken organizations years of planning to upgrade SharePoint or a new search engine. Now, it's quick and easy.

Constantly making improvements

One of the biggest advantages with the cloud is the constant ability to make improvements.

It takes so much less time to safely bring value to customers at a much more rapid cadence. Even small changes can compound very quickly, and we are able to get them into the customer's hands. This lets them take advantage of focusing on innovation investments.

Sometimes those aren't massive changes, but the nice thing is that if you roll out features every month or every week, small features compound very quickly. Our ability to get those into customers' hands for them to actually be taking advantage of it allows us to take the telemetry and signal to understand what's working and what are people actually using.

Better aligning our field teams to support customers

In the last couple of years, we chose to realign our sales teams to industry verticals in order to understand our customer's business better. Our teams now only handle retail or they only handle banking or they only handle pharmaceuticals. Then, we focused our teams around consumption instead of license sales. We wanted to help our enterprise customers adopt and consume and use cloud services so we changed the incentive models.

We have customer success managers as well as cloud solution architects that can spend time with an enterprise to help them understand, get trained better, and to be more successful.

We've tried to be very flexible around large customers who often have unique security needs or unique certification or indemnification or audit requirements. So we've also put together programs that can help with all of those. At the end of the day, we try to take the journey to the cloud through a technology approach, a knowledge approach, and an overall business approach. How do we really optimize that to enable our customers to be successful?

Automation improves security

The security benefits of moving to the cloud is perhaps one of the clearest for customers. Through the power of the cloud, Microsoft customers benefit from real-time detections and automations that are powered by the trillions of signals coming through the Microsoft Intelligent Security Graph. Through the insights and

"We're partnering with Zscaler to provide network as a service options that integrate with Azure and with Office 365 and the Microsoft Cloud more broadly."

real-time data process and the power of the cloud can we protect customers in seconds when we see an attack.

The automation and homogeneous nature of the cloud also empowers customers to streamline their environments versus traditional on-premise data centers fraught with different networking gear, different servers, different operating systems, different firmware, and different patching levels—all contributing to exponentially more maintenance and complexity. The nice thing about having a cloud-based system or a cloud infrastructure provider or a SaaS provider is it drives customers toward automation that helps them scale better. Manual processes that are slower and plagued by the potential for human error are simply not an option in the cloud. On top of all of that, at Microsoft, we can and do invest more in the security of our cloud infrastructure than our customers could do on their own. In this way, our customers can leverage our investments to their benefit. Finally, security is constantly changing. Hackers continue to get more sophisticated and the defenders must constantly work to keep up or get ahead of them.

If you think about the investment that we're making, there's a core set of services and solutions that we're building. Take, for example, with Azure Active Directory, we're providing identity as a service as part of Microsoft Cloud. On the networking side, we provide to our telco partners what we call Express Route, which enables direct network pipes between their facilities and ours. We're partnering with Zscaler to provide network as a service options that integrate with Azure and with Office 365 and the Microsoft Cloud more broadly.

Integrated offerings: Identity, Network, SaaS, and PaaS

I encourage CIOs to make the move to SaaS wherever possible. One of the benefits of SaaS is you constantly get innovations and updates and improvements. From a long-term ROI perspective, a SaaS solution that's always kept up to date, continuously improved, and which someone else can do the backup, the operations, and all the work-around, in the long run delivers much higher return on investment. That's partly why, when you look at Microsoft Cloud portfolio, all of those are delivered via SaaS.

Our goal with the Microsoft Cloud is to do both SaaS and infrastructure as a service, but more importantly, integrate the two. For instance, if you're doing custom data analytics you may have your users use a business intelligence SaaS solution like Power BI. You could then take data from your Office 365 systems and put it into a managed data warehouse on Azure. That in turn is delivered as a PaaS service, which uses custom AI and a custom set of platform services to make it richer. In that case, you have the benefits of both worlds, which is you're still heavily SaaS on a whole bunch of different dimensions, but you always have that flexibility to spin up a VM or to use a PaaS service to do something custom.

Data privacy, data residency, and GDPR compliance is a priority

We've done a couple things to help our enterprise customers with data privacy and compliance. We're committed to making sure our products and services are GDPR compliant and have made significant investments to redesign our systems and processes to meet its requirements at scale. We provide our customers with robust tools, backed up by contractual commitments, to help them with their compliance. Since this is a new regulation and we expect interpretations will change over time, we will constantly evaluate our products, services, and data uses as understanding of GDPR evolves.

GDPR has accelerated cloud migration in some cases as organizations realized it would simply be more efficient and less expensive to host their data in the Microsoft cloud where we can help them protect their customers' data and maintain GDPR compliance. We've been very clear about data residency and data sovereignty and guaranteeing when you move data into a Microsoft Cloud region, that data is stored in that region. You have control. From a contract perspective and from a legal perspective we guarantee your data residency and that when we move your data across borders it is done in compliance with applicable laws, and we are willing to put that in writing. That's been critical for European customers as well as customers elsewhere around the world in terms of having the confidence that they can actually trust their businesses with us.

Hybrid Cloud

We believe in hybrid and have approached it as an optimized state for a customer. The easier you can make it for people to link to the systems they already have and get value on day one, the faster they'll be successful and frankly the more they'll want to work with you. Hybrid is not just about making existing applications work. Think about IoT and how a manufacturer or someone who operates oil drilling platforms may want to take advantage of the cloud but cannot risk losing connectivity. We help them do compute locally or on the edge to provide that uptime while they may still use the cloud for data analytics or backup.

Hybrid solutions are not just for the past and for systems that are already built. It is also going to be the design footprint for new applications.

Artificial intelligence leverages data to run your business effectively

In many ways data is going to be the new digital currency. Every business is looking to find ways that they can use AI and data more effectively to transform their operations. And so we're on a path to build data and AI capabilities that can be used horizontally but also looking at how can I take my data inside Dynamics, my data inside Office, that's my data as an enterprise, and how can I actually use the AI and data services inside Azure to reason over it and run my business more effectively?

Have a trusted partner

One of the most important things is to have a trusted partner that you can work with to go down the cloud path. There will always be more that you can do if you're successful in your cloud journey, so having a trusted partner that can guide you along that path is essential.

"In many ways data is going to be the new digital currency."

The key is to just get started. Five years ago, cloud was still relatively new for a lot of enterprises, but we're now entering an adoption phase where the majority of new systems are now cloud based. Cloud has reached the mainstream and moving down that path is the right approach.

Amazon's Cloud Journey

Stephen Orban, General Manager, Amazon Web Services

"When customers are thinking about where they want to move their mission-critical and production IT workloads, they should consider which platform is going to have the most experience, and the best practices, to help them do that."

Stephen Orban, General Manager, Amazon Web Service

Amazon Web Services (AWS) gets credit for being early to the game. Stephen Orban, General Manager at AWS, writing in his book *Ahead in the Cloud* states, "I genuinely believe that cloud computing is the single most meaningful technology advancement in my lifetime." Stephen tells the story of Amazon's cloud transformation and how it scaled to meet unexpected demand.

In the words of Stephen Orban:

The software that Amazon used to run its retail website was massive and monolithic. Its size made it hard for the company to move as quickly as it wanted and to develop the new features it needed. Our teams began to trip over each other and, if somebody made a change and it broke the build, everybody else who had a change backed up behind it was delayed as well. Amazon made a deliberate move across the organization to transition into what we all know now as a service-oriented architecture (SOA). We broke up the software that ran retail into hundreds—and now even thousands—of services that all communicate with each other in a loosely coupled way via hardened APIs.

That idea also changed the way the engineering teams were organized. We call it a "two-pizza team" size, meaning that a team should be no larger than would consume two pizzas at one sitting. In this system, all the folks who were required to own and operate a service existed in one team, and they communicated with all the other teams by the APIs they published for the services.

That allowed us to move a lot quicker, but pretty soon we realized that a lot of these two-pizza teams were still spending a disproportionate amount of time managing the operating system, the databases, the storage, and the infrastructure that they were using.

So the founders of AWS, Andy Jassy and others, thought, "If Amazon is having this issue—even though we're really good at running a world-class data center and infrastructure—other companies must be having this problem, too." We saw that we could develop some services that we could use ourselves to make our teams faster, and that would make developers all over the world faster, as well.

That was the premise behind how AWS came to be. And what started off as a very small handful of simple storage, compute, and database options

Cloud Provider Journey | Amazon Web Services

back in 2006 has become a platform offering more than 125 services that range from compute, storage databases, and networking security, all the way up to DevOps, mobile tools, artificial intelligence, and machine-learning services. We also built a world-class team of customer support and account managers to help customers use the services and platforms so that they, too, can free more of their resources to focus on things that matter most to their customers.

Three factors that have contributed to AWS' growth

Jeff Bezos, our founder, would say that there are at least three things attributable to the company's growth. The first is that we're customer obsessed. If you translate that to AWS, 90% of our roadmap and the features and services that we've built over the last 12 years have been directly influenced by the things our customers have asked of us. It was our customers who requested a set of services that would make it easier to develop mobile apps. Machine learning and artificial intelligence are other examples. Those things are hard to build infrastructure for; things that we could do and provide as a service, such as SageMaker.

The second factor is that we like to invent new things. I think it's safe to say that AWS is largely known as the inventor of public cloud computing and other services.

And then, the third thing is that we are oriented for the long term. One of the things that Jeff says is that we're willing to be misunderstood for long periods of time. I think in 2006 when Amazon first launched a simple storage service, there were a lot of people who didn't understand it and thought maybe Amazon should stick to selling books. We continued to take a long-term view and believed that if we kept listening to customers and inventing features on their behalf, this could turn into something. Nobody had the audacity to predict it would become as big as it became.

The importance of resiliency

We build reliability, operational excellence, and security into our services from the very beginning. It's not a situation where we develop some feature or service and then, just before we're about to release it, we try to figure out how to make it reliable, durable, secure. We have a team of engineers across the business who think very deeply about these things throughout the process of designing our services.

As I mentioned, we listen to our customers and continue to add new features. So, as customers tell us that they need better reliability in one particular area or a new feature, we listen and try to follow very quickly with features that will meet those needs.

Another thing we think about is that we operate our services on a global scale with many, many different regions all over the world. Within each region, there are several availability zones, and within each availability zone, there are several data centers. We design our services across that global infrastructure so that we can build fault tolerance and redundancy into them. And then, of course, the service level agreements (SLAs) that we advertise on our services—we actually meet them.

Cloud Provider Journey | Amazon Web Services

We continue to scale to meet customer needs

At the moment, we have 55 availability zones inside 18 geographic regions covering the world. We've announced 12 more availability zones for four more regions in Bahrain, Hong Kong, Sweden, and another region in the U.S. for our government customers. It's called GovCloud, and it's used by millions of customers every single day.

Enterprise support fuels our customers' success

We have large sets of account teams that consist of account managers and solutions architects. The solutions architects are really the engineers who have a broad view of how our customers are using the platform, and they help them design, implement, and operate the things they're building on AWS.

We also have a large and fast-growing professional services team that consults on larger-scale migrations or digital transformation projects. To help customers on a longer-term basis, we have teams of support engineers and technical account managers with in-depth knowledge of how systems were designed and how they operate on our platform. As customers ramp up, these teams help customers optimize their workloads.

We've also developed a number of programs over the years that are designed to help customers achieve a particular business outcome. The best example I would give is a program that I built with my former team. Starting back in November of 2014, we created the migration acceleration program or MAP. The idea behind MAP was to serve those customers who were saying: *Okay, I get it. I'm doing all my new workloads on the cloud, but I have a lot of technical debt that I have accrued over the course of the last 10 or 20 or 50 years. I've got a number of data centers all over the world and I want to get out of these data centers, and I want to retire a lot of this technical debt so that I can focus more on doing the innovative things that my customers and my business really need.*

We built MAP to pull together all of the best practices around large-scale migrations to the cloud—those that involve thousands of applications at a time or dozens of data centers at a time. The best practices include those from our partner ecosystems, from our professional services teams, from our solutions architects, and from our customers themselves—all places where we can help a customer assess their portfolio, understand what's in it and all the dependencies. We have to know that this application talks to that application or database. Then, we build a business case so that the customer understands the financial implications of what a large-scale move to the cloud might mean. In short: connect the dots, then build a plan in which they can execute a really large migration.

A common theme we are seeing is customers moving 75% of their application portfolio to the cloud over the course of the next three years in an effort to save some tens of millions of dollars. They expect to increase developer productivity by anywhere between 30% and 70%.

These savings reflect what I accomplished when I was at Dow Jones, right before I joined Amazon. Our business case was across News Corp. We moved 75 percent of our infrastructure to the cloud over about a three-year period for a savings of $100 million a year. We were then able to devote that savings back into things that mattered to our business.

"A common theme we are seeing is customers moving 75% of their application portfolio to the cloud."

Cloud Provider Journey | Amazon Web Services

Building in privacy and GDPR

We look to build the necessary compliance framework into all of our services. We advertise which services support which compliance framework—GDPR or PCI or HIPAA or whatever the compliance framework may be. Through our various account teams, we also help customers to architect and build their applications so that they remain compliant with whatever security, regulatory, or privacy requirements that customer has.

In our business, we have a shared responsibility model. Where that line of responsibility is drawn depends on the service, so we're responsible for the security and the privacy of everything up and to a particular point. For example, for IaaS, we manage the facility, the actual physical instance, and the hypervisor, and then the customers decide which operating system they want to deploy and which software they want to put on top of that to run their application. So, they're responsible for everything from that layer above and we're responsible for everything below.

Picking a cloud service provider

If you believe as we do that a lot of that IT infrastructure over the course of the next decade is going to move to the cloud, it's not surprising that many of the large, traditional enterprise IT vendors are trying to build a replica of what AWS has built over the course of the last 12 years. There really is no compression algorithm for experience. Every day, we have more customers using more services on our platform, giving us more feedback, helping us see more ways where we can become operationally excellent and help them save money. While it may not be surprising that everybody's trying to build a replica, it is surprising how much of a head start they gave us.

When customers are thinking about where they want to move their mission-critical and production IT workloads, they should consider which platform is going to have the most experience, and the best practices, to help them do that.

Significant cost savings

We have yet to find a case where we couldn't save a customer money. I would say in lift-and-shift migration scenarios, where you're not substantially changing anything about the application, the savings can range anywhere from 25 to 40%. And when you start to think about a larger-scale architecture, where you move to microservices or serverless architectures—where you're only provisioning the resources that you need when you need them as opposed to over-provisioning servers like you would have had to do in a data center—the savings can be much more substantial than that. I've seen customers shave off 80% by moving to a serverless architecture.

One or many cloud service providers?

It's definitely not winner take all. There will continue to be multiple cloud providers, but it's a capital-intensive business, and I don't think that there will be dozens. I think there's going to be a small number. In my view—10 years from now, let's say—it's pretty hard to imagine that many companies will be running anything like the data center footprints they have today.

How Google is Building a Massively Scalable Cloud

Tariq Shaukat, President, Partner and Industry Platforms, Google Cloud

---

> *"Cloud, which originally started as a convenient way to get access to relatively elastic computing infrastructure, has really become a core engine of business growth and business transformation in many ways. It is not just a CIO and CTO conversation, but a CEO, board, and a line-of-business conversation."*

Tariq Shaukat, President, Partner and Industry Platforms, Google Cloud

---

Google too had built its own infrastructure to handle the vast loads of compute and data processing for its search engine, YouTube, and Gmail. It entered the cloud service business by introducing applications rather than raw storage or compute.

Tariq highlights how Google leveraged their internal treasure trove of state-of-the-art technology and externalized it in their journey to the cloud.

I am the President of Partner and Industry Platforms at Google Cloud, with responsibility for three main areas within the cloud organization here. One of those main areas is our strategic partnerships with the tech ecosystem; like those service providers who work with us on the cloud.

Google has always operated in a cloud-like environment. In fact, if you look at many of the technologies that are now foundational in the cloud, whether that is MapReduce or data analytics for data management purposes, or Kubernetes for container management purposes—the list goes on—these are all technologies that were developed and deployed inside of Google for the operations of Google.

We have seven different global applications that have over a billion users each. These require very high throughput and very low latency. We truly have been architecting in a cloud-oriented way since the very early days of the company. It was, therefore, logical to move into the cloud platform space, and into the G Suite cloud-based software space, as an extension of what we were already doing.

We already had the state-of-the-art technology being used internally at Google. What we had to do was externalize that. From a product standpoint, we needed to make it accessible and usable by companies that are not Google, and then we needed to build a go-to-market capability to acquire customers. That really was the journey. It started from a technology standpoint

Cloud Provider Journey | Google Cloud

and thinking about the capabilities needed to run Google Search, Google Maps, YouTube, etc., and then extending that to our customers.

I think, like many things at Google, there's a lot of innovation that happens across the whole company versus in a top-down manner. A lot of things start as the famous "20% project." Every engineer is encouraged to spend 20% of his or her time on projects outside of their regular scope. Our evolution to G Suite started with the consumer version of the apps that we had—Gmail, Docs, Slides, and Sheets. It was a set of grassroots initiatives and kept with the mission of Google to organize the world's information and make it universally accessible and useful. From that original heritage, it eventually grew into the small business realm and then enterprise world.

Within Google, we have different pieces that make up the cloud. There's G Suite, a highly secure and available cloud-native set of applications. Several large, traditional companies use this platform, including Airbus, Colgate-Palmolive, and Verizon. In addition, over four million smaller paying businesses use G Suite. And then there is Google Cloud Platform (GCP). This is a collection of dozens of different product offerings, including infrastructure service, compute network storage, data analytics, and machine learning.

Google has a large developer community that is mostly self-service: they come on and consume as they need, and stop consuming when they need to stop. That is how Snapchat, as an example, got started on GCP, and it's an important part of our business today.

Cloud, which originally started as a convenient way to get access to relatively elastic computing infrastructure, has really become a core engine of business growth and business transformation in many ways. It is not just a CIO and CTO conversation, but a CEO, board, and a line-of-business conversation.

When you're dealing in any enterprise and certainly any business context, security is critically important. Our network is a fundamental advantage—that low latency and performance we get operating inside of GCP—because we own so much of the fiber ourselves.

Selecting a cloud service provider

We always advise customers to use a strategic vendor. Besides the cloud vendor you choose, more important is how you choose to construct the architecture. You can go down the path of architecting in a way that's proprietary to one of the clouds that you would choose. Or you could go down the path of architecting so that you can run in multiple clouds, or in any cloud, or on-premises for that matter. So, we think the containerization movement, as an example, is a critically important decision that companies should be making. It determines the level of lock-in, the level of flexibility, and the level of tech debt that they're going to accumulate over the years.

Whether you are modernizing on-prem or you're moving to Google or you're moving to one of our competitors, we would recommend that you make a future-proof decision on architecture as opposed to what may seem like the most convenient near-term decision.

"We find CTOs and CIOs are used to thinking about security in an on-prem environment."

Minimizing lock-in is something we hear time and time again from customers. I would encourage people to look at how much the different clouds embrace open-source technology. That's important not just from a lock-in standpoint, but from a security standpoint.

Security is obviously critically important. It needs to be front and center. We find CTOs and CIOs are used to thinking about security in an on-prem environment. They think about how to build walls around their systems. Almost by definition, when you move into the cloud, the walls disappear, and you need a different security model. You want a company that will support and innovate and is really investing in those security models.

Almost every CEO and CIO that I talk to right now is thinking about how their business is going to change in the next 10 years. Years ago we talked about "digital transformation." Today we're hearing more and more about "data-driven transformation," the idea that one of the most valuable assets you have as a company is your data. Traditionally, those data assets have been locked in silos and you couldn't get access to them. You couldn't join the data. You didn't have a full view of your supply chain or your customers. It's important to figure out where can you get the most value out of the data that you have.

The big three are not alone

There are competitors to AWS, Google Cloud Platform, and Azure. Oracle Cloud Platform, for instance, is available in 17 data centers distributed across North and South America, Asia, and Europe. Citrix Cloud for hosting remote desktops was introduced in 2015. IBM SmartCloud can be purchased as a public cloud, private cloud, or hybrid cloud. IBM continues to invest in its platform and services offerings, as evidenced through the recent acquisition of RedHat.[11]

VMware has had an important role to play in the world of cloud. Its Hypervisor was the first commercially successful virtualization technology and is the basis of many enterprise private clouds. VMware introduced its own IaaS offering, vCloud Air, in May 2013.

Selecting the Right Provider

AWS has a head start on the competition, building out its suite of cloud services since 2005. They offer a broad range of services and platform configuration options and have a rich partner ecosystem. Their services are built to be enterprise-friendly so that they will appeal to CIOs as well as its core audience of developers.

Azure excels in enterprise-readiness and is a natural fit for organizations that already use Microsoft applications and systems in-house such as Office 365, Windows Server, and Active Directory, and can help these organizations transition easily to the cloud. While both AWS and Azure have PaaS capabilities, Microsoft has a strength in this area.

---

11 IBM to acquire software company Red Hat for $34 billion: https://www.reuters.com/article/us-red-hat-m-a-ibm/ibm-to-acquire-software-company-red-hat-for-34-billion-idUSKCN1N20N3

Google Cloud is popular with cloud-native organizations and has a strong presence within the open source community. However, they are a newer entrant and have traditionally struggled to break into the enterprise market. A key strength of Google Cloud is their innovation and leadership in the areas of machine learning with their internal expertise in AI and TensorFlow.

In many cases, most companies have a multi-cloud strategy and are using multiple vendors. There are several benefits to this approach including mitigating vendor lock-in, ability to leverage best of breed capabilities, cost reduction, and increased application reliability.

Chapter 7 Takeaways

Cloud adoption is fast becoming the de facto option for new services. After many years of being considered hype and an upcoming trend, the cloud is now a tested and tried option for modern enterprise IT. In fact, in many cases it is considered a business imperative and a critical requirement for enterprise agility. Organizations that fail to acknowledge the benefits may soon find themselves left behind by both their users and their competitors.

Some considerations when selecting the cloud service and provider for your business needs:

- Evaluate the cloud service based on availability in region and services offered; ascertain your organization's risk profile and map the required security controls to the available service to identify gaps and determine mitigation steps.

- Identify responsibility splits between your organization, the cloud service provider, and the application vendor for SaaS applications so a clear responsibility matrix can be outlined.

- Understand the service terms and conditions offered by the cloud service provider and be aware of any additional regulatory, compliance, and legislative clauses that you may have to comply with.

- Ensure that the service provider you select is a trusted partner that you can work with on your cloud journey. Understand their support and operations model and ensure that this aligns with your end user and business goals.

In the next chapter, we will discuss how the modern IT organization and C-Suite are evolving to adapt to the mega-trends, and to embark on cloud transformation.

THE CIO MANDATE

Chapter 8: The Role of the CIO is Evolving

This chapter lays the foundation, addresses the evolving landscape of enterprise IT and the CIO mandate, the challenges they face today in future-proofing their corporate networks while delivering technology innovation and business agility, and shines the light on the pivotal roles they play in transforming their organizations.

Chapter 9: CIO Journeys

In this chapter we showcase three leading enterprise transformation journeys through candid interviews from their IT leaders that cut across a wide range of sectors, business and technical goals, company sizes, and challenges.

CHAPTER 8

The Role of the CIO is Evolving

"We've got to go faster."

Bruce Lee, Former CIO, Fannie Mae

Adapt or Disrupt

Enterprise digital transformation is upon us and its impact on IT and the business is imminent. As Michael Day, CIO of Cannery Casino Resort states, "Change is inevitable. Change is upon you now, and more is coming. You cannot prevent it, and you cannot slow it down."[12]

With that emerges a new kind of IT leader with transformational skills—one that becomes the bridge between the business and IT. More and more enterprises today rely on their CIOs to successfully navigate their organizations through continuous change, making this role more challenging and critical than ever. Historically, the heavy emphasis for the CIO role was placed on technical skills but this is now rapidly changing to encompass a more strategic mandate.

---

12 The Changing Role of the CIO: https://www.cioreview.com/contributors/michael-day/15203

As the C-Suite gears up to out-innovate their competition, CIOs are invariably being positioned as the function most responsible for moving innovation initiatives forward within their organizations.[13] To achieve this, the CIO's mindset must change—from one of controls to one of risk. The illustration below summarizes how IT leaders traditionally controlled all aspects of IT services. With the advent of cloud and mobility, all of that has changed.

Figure 8.1 The change from control-based to risk-based thinking

The role of the CIO now spans a broader mandate, shifting from a delivery executive to business executive, i.e., from controlling costs and re-engineering processes to driving revenue and exploiting data.[14] Delivering business growth, driving organization-wide digital transformation, and improving the enterprise's risk posture with the rapid increase in cybersecurity threats are cited to be some of the top priorities for CIOs today.[15]

13 KPMG: The Changing Landscape of Disruptive Technologies, Tech Hubs forging new hubs to outpace competition; p.13: https://assets.kpmg.com/content/dam/kpmg/ca/pdf/2018/03/tech-hubs-forging-new-paths.pdf
14 Gartner: Mastering the New Business Executive Job of the CIO Insights From the 2018 CIO Agenda Report: https://www.gartner.com/imagesrv/cio-trends/pdf/cio_agenda_2018.pd
15 ibid.

Barriers to Innovation

As we establish the organizational impetus to innovate and the role of the CIO in making this a reality, why aren't more and more enterprise CIOs committing to this digital journey? The reality is that the majority of CIOs are faced with an array of organizational challenges that become barriers to innovation and impede their ability to make this shift. These barriers can range from existing organizational silos, to legacy processes, to internal cultural resistance to change, to the lack of innovative thinking throughout the organization.[16] In many cases, CIOs are being tasked with raising the Titanic with little strategic, digital, and organization support and know-how.

Become a Digital Enabler

CIOs today must face the challenge of embracing disruption proactively and with a carefully formulated game plan, rather than adapting incrementally. As the adage goes, "disrupt or be disrupted."

The first step to becoming a digital disruptor is to challenge the current mindset and embrace a culture of innovation.

Gartner defines the five key traits of a digital disruptor as follows:[17]

1. Thrive despite uncertainty. A disruptive digital leader understands and embraces the idea that uncertainty is inevitable. They explore what is technologically possible, how changes will disrupt the markets and the risk-reward trade-offs, and they establish a plan that allows for change and evolution.

---

16 Harvard Business Review: Driving Digital Transformation: New Skills for Leaders, New Role for the CIO; p4: https://hbr.org/sponsored/2015/03/driving-digital-transformation-new-skills-for-leaders-new-role-for-the-cio
17 Gartner: Leading Through Digital Disruption - Gartner insights on spotting and responding to digital disruption; p.16: https://www.gartner.com/imagesrv/books/digital-disruption/pdf/digital_disruption_ebook.pdf

2. Focus on ideas that leapfrog ahead. All decisions need to be rooted in the end goal or mission. This demands a risk-tolerant mindset and a true digital leader is driven by the challenge and potential for creating net-new business value by harnessing breakthrough technology.

3. Select your digital-era lever. Digital leaders look beyond distractions. Their goal is to become a pioneer and to sustain a long-term investment to secure a position as a leader. They do this by selecting a lever and focus on making it a core competency of the company.

4. Start, experiment, learn, iterate. Digital leaders understand well-grounded strategic bets based on expected business outcomes and digital levers need to be the focus of the company. They take an experiment-driven learning loop approach to inform actions rather than waiting for absolute clarity before proceeding.

5. Innovate faster than others. In a digital era rich in disruption, it's a given that companies must innovate faster than their competitors. By actively championing and role-modeling a culture of innovation and creativity they encourage risk-taking and discovery across all levels of the organization.

General Electric Company

Office 365 Migration at Scale

Company:	General Electric	Revenue:	$122 billion
Sector:	Conglomerate	Employees:	300,000
Driver:	Larry Biagini	Countries:	170
Role:	Former VP & CTO	Locations:	8,000

Company IT Footprint: GE is a global name and has been an icon of technology innovation for well over a century. At the time of writing, there were about 9,000 IT employees and another 15,000 contractors at GE. They maintained an application portfolio of around 8,000 applications, and were distributed across 45,000 compute nodes. Their IT infrastructure was spread across 300,000 employees that sat in 170 countries around the world.

"The modern CIO has to understand where the business is trying to go, because if a business isn't growing, it's dying and everyone out there knows that they're at threat from digital companies."

Larry Biagini, former Vice President and Chief Technology Officer, General Electric Company

---

In the pre-cloud world, everything inside the defined corporate network was considered to be good, and everything outside was potentially harmful. So the game was to protect the inside from the potentially bad on the outside. Unfortunately, there is no inside and outside anymore. Larry Biagini was formerly the Vice President and Chief Technology Officer at General Electric. In the next part of this chapter, he shares his perspectives on GE's cloud transformation journey during his tenure. He also highlights how the C-Suite is evolving, and how the role of the modern CIO is shifting from technology-first to business-first today, requiring them to transition from control-based thinking to a risk-based mindset.

In the words of Larry Biagini:

I retired from GE in 2015 after spending 26 years in various roles ranging from the CIO of a business unit to global CISO, as well as the global CTO. In 2010 it became very obvious to me and others that more and more activity was happening outside our corporate environment than inside. This was beyond activities like personal web browsing; we were doing more and more business over the internet. We were using software as a service applications to actually make our business more efficient via interactions with our suppliers and our customers.

We also had product and software engineers putting stuff in AWS or Azure to quickly try things out and so it became very clear that we had to re-evaluate how we were managing security to protect our environment. The old model was that everything inside was good, everything outside was potentially bad. So the game was to protect the inside from the potentially bad on the outside. Unfortunately, there was no inside and outside anymore. There were just people using devices on an available network trying to get their jobs done. The more walls we put up and the more security policies we put in place to try to protect our network, the more people found ways around it and the less visibility we had into what they were doing.

Protecting "the network" no longer works

Counterintuitively, by trying to protect the network, we were actually making the corporate network more vulnerable because we couldn't see what people were doing when they were not on our network.

"The old model was that everything inside was good, everything outside was potentially bad."

We couldn't prevent them 100% of the time from doing certain things that could have security consequences and our users were dissatisfied with the way security was trying to prevent them from getting their jobs done. For example, we had global policies in place that said things like sexual content needs to be blocked. Makes sense, but classification of content is not a science and we had researchers in our healthcare business being denied access to sites that had to do with cancer research. Trying to set up a policy based on where a user was in the network to allow the healthcare folks to look at breast cancer research, which may be misclassified as sexual content, while at the same time not allowing that same thing to happen in our finance business was almost impossible to do.

People were finding ways around it. They'd come in, they'd turn off their Wi-Fi connection and use 4G or LTE, so ultimately we were not doing our job because we were preventing our end users from doing theirs.

User mobility breaks the traditional networking and security paradigm

Our organization was already widely distributed, and we were starting to see that more and more of our people were working remotely—they were out at customer sites, on windmills, and visiting oil rigs. They were out doing their jobs and they were off our network. So this idea of protecting the corporate network soon became deciding to only put the pieces of the network that are so crucial to us behind a perimeter that we will never allow them to be connected to the internet, and treating everybody as if they're on an open network connection—treat it like an untrusted network. Our goal was to protect our users no matter where they were and that's when we started thinking about simply moving our proxy into the cloud. The proxy acted as a security gateway between our internal corporate network and the internet.

User mobility necessitates change and one of the first things we did was move our proxies and gateways to the cloud.

Cloud security enables user-centric policy enforcement

Moving our security gateway into the cloud gave us one clear benefit. Now we could actually tie policies, both a security policy and a compliance policy, to an individual user no matter where they were in the world.

Regardless of the network they were on, the user would always get the same experience. It wasn't dependent upon whether you were sitting in Atlanta, New York, or San Ramon, California. Once the security gateway was in the cloud and the policy followed the user, we had happier users.

"Now we could actually tie policies, both a security policy and a compliance policy, to an individual user no matter where they were in the world."

Delivering a rich user experience while maintaining visibility

So the first big win for us was user satisfaction. The ability to deliver a consistent user experience—both from a performance standpoint, and a policy standpoint. And that made a big difference in the way that our users thought about our security team.

From a security perspective we now had visibility into what everybody was doing wherever they were. There was no concept of on-net or off-net anymore. We could see if the user was home, at a Starbucks, or in the office. We could apply a policy but we could also get security visibility into what they were doing. So the chances of a user being off-net, getting infected because they weren't protected by the network controls that we had in place and then coming back on-net and causing a problem went down drastically.

If we can kick everybody off the corporate network and they're going to the internet through a cloud security gateway, that's fine, as we're protected and can apply compliance policies. But the reality is that the user has to get back onto the corporate network to run applications that are in our data center. The traditional solution was a network VPN connection, but that broke our model. If we allowed them to come back on the network via VPN, we were opening our corporate network to whatever evil lay on the other side of the VPN.

We ended up developing our own solution, My Apps, that allowed a user anywhere to run any internal web-based application without being on the corporate network. Basically we validated and authenticated the user and we validated and authenticated the device. And if both of those passed the test and you had a policy that you were able to run that application, you run that application wherever you were.

We were talking to Zscaler, our cloud proxy provider at the time, and we saw great use for it as we were doing acquisitions and divestitures. We were doing an acquisition where we knew that the acquired company was compromised and it would take us years to fix it. We used My Apps to give the acquired company's users access to GE applications and vice versa—GE people accessed the acquired company's applications without ever connecting the networks together.

This was a time saver, a money saver, and obviously better security posture for us.

Since then, Zscaler has introduced Zscaler Private Access (ZPA) to do the same. ZPA is much more robust than what we built ourselves and much more integrated in the cloud, but the same premise holds true: you can't secure a network that allows users on it. Because networks don't really get attacked, you attack users who have network access. After that it's pretty much game over. Most organizations have a flat network where once you're in you can go anywhere. Those who have tried to segment those networks at the network level have failed miserably. I know because we tried as well, and it's just way too complicated, especially in a large organization.

Connect users to applications not networks

So the solution is really to make sure that the right user on the right device gets access to the right services regardless of the network they're on. If you can do that you can kick all your users off your corporate network. And you're 100 times more secure.

If you think about it logically, you don't own the network because as soon as you connect to the internet, you've lost complete control. It doesn't matter if you're a two-person shop or 200,000 person shop—the more connections, or any connections, you have gives you a loss of control. If you have users that have things like laptops, or iPads, or iPhones, they're not always going to be on the network that you want to control.

Your employees are going to be doing business, they're going to be at risk from infections, ransomware, and things like that. Many organizations only have network security, which means you are secure only in your office and on the corporate network. When users go home, they have no protection, are at risk and get infected with ransomware. They come back the next day, they plug into the corporate network, and that ransomware will now infect the entire corporate network.

"Make sure that the right user on the right device gets access to the right services regardless of the network they're on."

Take the same scenario where that person could do their job every single day no matter whether they're at home or at the office, and not be on the network that you care about. They'll still possibly get infected with ransomware possibly, but if they do, the damage is limited, because the network they're on is not the corporate network that you care about. It's the internet. The only thing they can affect is the person sitting next to them at home, but it can't spread across your internal company network because your internal network never hosts that user.

It's an enormous shift in thinking but it's the only shift that makes sense. For everybody who's trying to secure their entire network from bad things happening, the next question you will need to ask them is how big their exception list is? Because everybody has exceptions. They may say they have a policy that says you can't do these five things, except for the CEO who has privileges to do so. What you find when you start peeling back the onion is that their network protections are porous, never mind the network being porous. The network protections themselves are porous by design.

If you want to go in front of your board and say that you can prevent 95% of bad things happening to your organization by doing one thing and one thing only, tell them you could turn off accepting external emails into your organization. With just that one thing, you will create an environment where you are so well protected from anything bad happening that they'll love you immediately. On the other hand, not accepting unknown emails from unknown parties is a terrible business decision.

So, this is the discussion that you have. Why don't you just block email? And the response will be that you can't, because people need to communicate with the outside world. Well, the same is true outside of email. People need to communicate with the outside world. They work outside of the organization so they understand that this is the risk that you have to live with, and design your solutions differently.

Make your data center an application destination like a public cloud

We had potential customers who told me they had a plan to get all their applications into the cloud by 2020. My response to them was that this just wasn't going to happen. It just doesn't make business sense to move all your applications, and if you don't know it now, you'll know it when you start to move some of these applications.

"The first step in digital transformation is understanding that what we built for the last 20 years doesn't apply."

What's more important is that your data center becomes part of the cloud infrastructure and treat your own applications as cloud applications whether you move them or not. By leveraging My Apps, which we built at GE, we were able to turn internal applications into something that looked like an SaaS application without ever moving them to AWS, Google Cloud, or Azure. Those platforms are enablers for certain things, but this doesn't mean that you can't transform yourself by continuing to host your own applications.

I get intrigued when people say they're going to have a hybrid data center. No, you're going to have a hybrid network. Just turn your data center into a destination for the people that are supposed to use it and you don't have to do anything else. Now you may want to because it may be more efficient to run certain workloads in a cloud environment or it may become more efficient to rewrite some of your applications so they work better with some

CTO Journey | General Electric Company

of the capabilities that AWS and Azure provide, but the reality is that's not the first step in digital transformation.

The first step in digital transformation is understanding that what we built for the last 20 years doesn't apply anymore. Right, wrong, or indifferent, it just doesn't apply.

Security needs to shift from a control- to risk-based framework

Let's talk about organizational impact. If you think about it, a security team was always about running and cleaning up the latest mess, and if we suggest that the mess is going away, it leaves an organization wondering why it has a security team.

What they should be worried about is what the risks to their organization are and identifying those risks and making sure they are mitigated appropriately. For instance, we did a risk analysis on our entire organization. We asked the CEOs to explain the risk to their business, because everything can't be protected but we do want to protect what's most important. Pretty much everybody came back with intellectual property as the number one risk.

You know what? The intellectual property in a washing machine or a light bulb has a lifespan until the day you ship it to Home Depot or Lowes. Then it's out there and can be completely copied by anyone. Some of the intellectual property in an aircraft engine will decide whether you're in the engine business for the next 20 years or not. Yes, both assets are valuable intellectual property and we would like to protect them, but where are we going to really spend our effort? Not on figuring out how not to lose a sock in a dry-

CTO Journey | General Electric Company

er, but how not to allow competitors to take that one sliver of technology that we think is going to differentiate us over the next 20 years in aviation.

The security people must turn into people who understand risk—understand where their highest risks are and put their mitigations in place that allow those highest risks to not actually occur. In our organization we called them "crown jewels." They were so important to the organization that we were going to put so many controls on them, and invariably impact the productivity of the people who needed access.

We made sure that when users were accessing those systems, or that data, or those services, they had no email access and they were not connected to the internet. It wasn't a classified network but we were separating it from the rest of the network, an extra step to ensure that even if something bad happened to the network, it would never impact any other part of network. And our security team was looking at it 24/7, because it was that important for us.

Developing a proactive risk-based mindset

In the near future, security teams will need to turn into hunters to understand if they are being targeted. They will need to turn into risk leaders to understand where the risks are to your organization. They will also need to turn into knowledge experts when people start to move stuff into cloud services and understand how to implement policies in a secure manner.

Application development: traditional vs cloud-native

The CIOs too have a couple of challenges in this new paradigm. The first challenge is to manage expectations and to guide the conversation about

CTO Journey | General Electric Company

the difference between digital and cloud. Because CEOs and boards hear, "We have to go cloud." What the CIO has to do is understand how to give the business the tools it needs to get the business growing and that cloud is a part of that strategy, but it is not the only thing.

Second, the modern CIO has to understand the capabilities of their organization and most of them will realize quickly that they don't have the right talent in place to make this digital transformation. They have good people who have been worried about technology for the last 10, 15, 20 years, and what we're saying here is that the technology is still important but the technology is actually changing. If you're a network jockey and we decide to shrink the network so it's not relevant anymore, the role and the need for you is going to change. On the other hand, if you're a good network admin and you are moving applications off to AWS or Azure or Google Cloud, this will present different problems, so get yourself versed in what those issues are going to be.

If you're on the application side and think you're going to write an application the same way you did for the data center and allow it to run well in AWS, you're fooling yourself. It's a different skill set. "Lifting and Shifting" applications from on-premises to the cloud more often than not leads to disappointing results. You have to write apps differently. You have to think about them differently, you have to understand interaction between that cloud, other clouds, your users, and your data center. This is not what application people have done traditionally. Application teams get requirements from their functional users, they implement those functional requirements and everyone's happy.

Developing an in-depth knowledge of the technology stack

But now application teams have to understand much more of the technology stack: the databases, what they're using, the network connectivity between AWS and maybe the data center, the security protocols, the authentication protocols. Application people never had to worry about that—they always left it up to the infrastructure group because the infrastructure group managed the infrastructure. But you don't own the infrastructure anymore. Now what?

My number one tip is to bring in a small team that has done this before. Pick a couple of applications that you think are good candidates for moving out of your data center into the public cloud and let that team do it. Seed some of your developers who know the functionality with that team, let them learn the tools and techniques, let them see how it can be done, why it should be done and in many cases why it shouldn't be done. I think that gets the whole organization moving in the right direction.

If you show a few successes early on, both from a cost and a functionality standpoint, then you can get application teams, your network teams, and your infrastructure teams to recognize that they were part of that success. It encourages them to want to continue the success, and to know that they are capable to take on their own projects without continuing to hire people from the outside.

The roles of CIO, CTO, and CISO are changing

It's not just the CIO, it's the CTO, and the CISO as well. If you look at the three main roles, which are CIO, CTO, and CISO, the CIO shifts from technolo-

CTO Journey | General Electric Company

gy first to business first. Understand what your business actually needs, understand what your business wants, understand how your business operates and find the best technology solutions to allow that to happen, whether you own them or not.

The modern CIO has to understand where the business is trying to go, because if a business isn't growing, it's dying, and everyone out there knows that they're at threat from digital companies. He or she has to also understand what the company's doing, where its threats are, where its opportunities are, whether there is any white space that this new digitally connected world can allow them to take advantage of.

The CTO has to shift from architecting corporate networks to embracing the fact that you can't control everything, but you should know your users, you should know your devices, and you can control what they access. Don't think you have to build it because you can't. Don't think that your solutions are the only solutions that people are going to use.

And the CISO has to shift from security and controls to risk and enablement. If you could look at Salesforce today, it was first introduced in the organization not by IT, but by Sales. Why? Because it filled a need that IT couldn't address. And it was all done under the radar and then IT stepped in and said, look we're embracing cloud because we're using Salesforce. If it were up to most IT organizations they would've said no, we can build it ourselves, just give us the requirements.

And take a step back and think about any organization today. If you're able to build an HR system from scratch would any organization say, "Yes, I want to do that?" Absolutely not. If you had to build a CRM system, would you do it? The answer is absolutely not. If you had to build an expense system would you do it? Absolutely not.

We have large organizations out there who are running their own internal systems that need to start asking themselves the question of when is the appropriate time to tip the balance, to take the internal HR system that has been customized to hell and turn it over to Workday, for example? When is the appropriate time to take the manufacturing system and move it into NetSuite? It may not be today, but if you're not asking a question every single day, you're going to miss that point where you should've said, "Now's the time to do it."

The CIO has to educate their functional users that they are not going to get every bell and whistle they want and that they had. But instead, they get speed, they get accessibility, they get lower cost, and they get faster functionality introduction.

"The CISO has to shift from security and controls to risk and enablement."

Chapter 8 Takeaways

In the new world of cloud, CIOs are no longer providers of IT services, they are enablers of business services—the services that can make businesses more competitive and agile. Review the following list of the new ways a CIO, CTO, CDO, or a CISO should be thinking:

The new CIO/CTO/CDO:

- Focus on growth. Go fast—speed is the new currency
- Move from an IT shop to a "Digital Enabler"
- Be honest with your board about technology debt
- Address your legacy environment head-on
- Embrace the cloud, but thoughtfully for the right applications
- The internet is the new corporate network. Transform your legacy network to a direct-to-cloud architecture.

The new CISO:

- Stop talking security with your board. Focus on risk.
- Create a risk assessment and risk appetite so that the business has a means to make decisions
- Separate your critical assets from the consumers of those assets (don't put users and servers on the same network)
- Get identity right. Invest in identity and access management.
- Securing the network is no longer relevant. Connecting users to their applications securely irrespective of the network should be the goal.

CHAPTER 9

CIO Journeys

―――――――――――――――――――――――――――――――――――――――

"It's a new world. Don't take all of your old approaches with you. You can't assume that there's any physical choke point that's bringing everything back to a corporate enterprise perimeter and analyzing things. You have to understand what a true virtual, software-defined architecture looks like. When you understand that, you can understand how to move to the cloud securely."

Jim Reavis, Co-founder & CEO, Cloud Security Alliance

―――――――――――――――――――――――――――――――――――――――

From these innovators' stories a common thread emerges; one of early discovery of how the cloud provides distinct advantages, be they financial or in extending capabilities through greater IT agility, a faster pace of innovation, and lower costs. This is followed by the stage at which these organizations adopted a cloud-first strategy, which means one should always evaluate cloud options first. This mindset opens up the world of cloud transformation and leads to competitive and financial gains for all of the IT visionaries you find in this book. Along the way, these organizations discovered that they needed a cloud-delivered security layer to accomplish their goals.

We've compiled three additional cloud transformation journeys in this chapter.

Great-West Life

Accelerating the Financial Services Sector to the Cloud

Company:	**Great-West Life**	Revenue:	**$30 billion**
Sector:	**Financial Services**	Employees:	**24,000**
Driver:	**Philip Armstrong**	Countries:	**4**
Role:	**CIO**		

Company IT Footprint: GWL is the oldest insurance brand in Canada, and they have major subsidiaries in the United States, Ireland, the UK, and Germany. Of their 24,000 global employees, 3,200 are in information technology.

"And technology transformation does not happen in a vacuum. There are cultural and economic changes to consider."

Philip Armstrong, Chief Information Officer, Great-West Life

Great-West Life (GWL) is a holding company of multiple insurance and financial management firms. In all of their programs, it administers 1.2 trillion dollars in assets. Philip Armstrong is the Chief Information Officer at GWL. In this next journey, he describes GWL's journey to the cloud.

Since joining GWL in 2016, my challenge has been to reinvigorate our brands in the face of changing technology and communications channels to our customers. Every day, we must help our clients use their benefits or their pension programs to realize their financial dreams.

As an established company, we have everything from 1970s-era mainframes, which can't be beat for cost-effectiveness, to artificial intelligence (AI). So I have to ask: "How do we take that spread of technology and perform open heart surgery to improve it?" And technology transformation does not happen in a vacuum. There are cultural and economic changes to consider.

I have been in technology since I left school. I have worked in 40 countries and have lived through every hype cycle. But despite the hype, cloud is impacting the way we all do business. If you are like me, you are moving parts of your business to the cloud.

"How do we take that spread of technology and perform open heart surgery to improve it?"

At GWL, we are pursuing a hybrid model. We have five data centers and will continue to use them. We will use appropriate cloud providers. In some cases, where cloud does not make sense, workloads are moving back from the cloud. I think of the cloud as a fantastic tool for augmentation.

Modernizing through digital transformation

We are on a journey to refresh our brand. We are looking at robotics, process automation, and AI. We want to provide all of our services in the language our customers choose. We are transforming how people think about our business and how to plan for problems we don't even know about yet.

In Canada, 50% of our workforce is made up of millennials. Without a doubt, they have a different risk tolerance. Consumers are becoming increasingly tech-savvy. Our entire business is changing, from our base infrastructure to our products and service channels—voice, text, websites, or other means (Alexa, Google Home). New ways to connect with our customers are popping up all over the place.

Customers do not care if they came in over one channel last week and another this week. They expect us to know about those transactions. People now expect a certain level of technology from their providers. At GWL, we have to meet those expectations.

We work with thousands of financial planners and independent agents. We have to support them with technology that is easy to use and does not interfere with their current business processes.

SaaS adoption and beyond

Like most companies, we have gone through stages of transformation. We rapidly transitioned to Salesforce for customer engagement, Concur for expense reporting, and SuccessFactors for human resources. These are discrete functions that are easy to move to the cloud without disrupting our core business.

CIO Journey | Great-West Life

But there are architectural patterns you need to know about. When the cloud first became popular, some of our business units were excited for all the wrong reasons.

From the adoption of these discrete applications, we matured over the last two years. We started in the United States by moving workloads to Amazon East and West and Amazon was slow to open data centers in Canada. Our organization did a significant foray into AWS, and we had big decisions to make about whether to invest in data centers and recovery centers or whether our users and needs were the best fit for the cloud. We have been on that journey for about two years.

"Another advantage is that large cloud providers have invested in security."

Why has it taken so long? We wanted to do it right. We went through each of our applications. We hired specialized talent from Silicon Valley. We re-engineered to take advantage of cloud benefits like monitoring and elasticity. And we spent a lot of time getting ready.

We are looking at IaaS for end-of-the-month processing peaks, when we need extreme amounts of compute power. We have found that it is not true that cloud is always cheaper. One lesson learned was that moving to the cloud means you are transporting a lot more data. It's cheap to bring it in, very expensive to pull it out. It can cost you a fortune in data transfer expense.

Our largest IT suppliers—Cisco, IBM, and Oracle—have been gradually pushing their preferred environment, the cloud. That has a financial impact. It shifts your IT budget from predictable, contracted costs to a subscription model where expenses are variable. That shifts your budgets around. The accounting department complains about how lumpy your spending is. It impacts financial planning. One way we addressed that is by investing in Apptio. It measures usage, so I can cost out the technology in my data center and keep a close eye on who is spending what on cloud resources. And yes, it is cloud-based.

Another advantage is that large cloud providers have invested in security. More often than not, breaches are an internal mistake rather than some flaw in the way cloud infrastructure is architected.

Building the workforce

The shift to the cloud is a big cultural and training disruption, and you have to go through massive education for internal users. It's important to look at different departments and how people collaborate.

When it comes to moving a large organization, cloud transformation is 70% cultural and 30% technical.

Getting experienced cloud resources is difficult. Most companies are transitioning, are in the cloud, or have a hybrid. When you start to move to the cloud, you need developers that can develop applications in the cloud and you are paying a premium for toolkits, which are changing rapidly. If you are looking for someone with three to four years of in-depth cloud experience, then it is an arms race. You train them, and then they leave for a higher salary.

The other problem is the number of clouds. Spin up a public cloud instance; it drops down to AWS, then to my own data center. Between the clouds, you are actually going into the internet. You have to find people with multi-cloud experience to architect all of that.

You need financial people who can monitor usage, and DevOps people who can extend their knowledge into cloud. You also need cybersecurity people who need a whole host of skill sets. All of these skill sets are very expensive.

We have had a very deliberate strategy of partnering with large tech companies and leverage good professional services arrangements with them.

Should internal applications move to the cloud?

There are two schools of thought on moving workloads to the cloud. The companies that are starting their cloud journey look at obvious workloads. They have progressed to: "I am going to understand the benefits and cherry pick my internal apps to move to the cloud." Do they need elasticity to support a variable workload? Do they need the availability and easy access? Can they take advantage of the built-in security?

The other school of thought is that legacy applications are going to take a lot of money to move. Is there a hybrid approach that does not require complete rewrites? Keep in mind that if you do the hybrid approach, you will have some users going to the cloud and others who will be routed to your existing data centers. It is still early days in big organizations. Many are not ready to drop the VPN and authentication tokens. It's getting there, though.

Now we are starting to hear about large companies partnering to drop stacks into your data center. Cisco and Microsoft have partnered to drop an Azure stack in the data center, if I want it in-house, for whatever reason. That allows me to virtually "run it in the cloud."

I get exasperated when I hear CIOs say they are moving everything to the cloud. I have five mainframes. We view these as so cost effective, I doubt they will ever move to the cloud.

Securing it all

I am a believer in defense in depth, so I will have overlapping security capabilities. We have different types of detonation chambers in the cloud. We are using Zscaler for web traffic and Proofpoint for email. That will filter less sophisticated threats, the everyday burden of a constant flood of attacks. Therefore, volumes of incidents are reduced drastically.

We have very sophisticated appliances for application firewall defenses. As you drill your way into our data center, we use firewalls from multiple vendors. We are shifting to Microsoft Windows 10 and use Active Directory and Intune for mobile device management. We also have a privileged user management system for server access and track alerts in an SIEM (security information and event management). We have a large cybersecurity team, and we are under pressure to deliver on the promise of all this technology by ensuring that security is done right.

Partners and financial advisors can be a problem. Some work directly for us, so we can control their desktops and monitor their activity. Then we have people who have a commercial agreement with us, but own their own infrastructure and hardware.

"I am a believer in defense in depth, so I will have overlapping security capabilities."

CIO Journey | Great-West Life

What we try to do with them is give them tools that they can access securely via Zscaler Internet Access. You have to look at how they are accessing your applications, data stores, and tools before deciding how to protect those elements.

Complete independents can also sell our products. You have to ensure they come through routes you can secure. What we have found is you cannot stop everything, so you need these multiple levels of defense. You cannot monitor and measure everything, so you have to apply the more sophisticated technology, like AI, so your team can be freed up to focus on the important things.

The bad guys are starting to use AI to package their malware. They want to be able to bypass the sandbox technology everyone is deploying to catch their malware.

Zscaler saw the writing on the wall. The difference with Zscaler is they can inspect traffic inline. Detonation chambers have been around a long time, but they run in a virtual environment, and the sophisticated stuff detects the virtual environment and goes to sleep. Zscaler has built its own environment without the standard virtual machines, so the malware detonates and is detected.

One of the great things about working with cloud vendors is if I get infected by something, and I show the vendors what I have seen, they will learn from it. Then they implement protection in real time into the cloud.

An example of our security working is that we had no issues with Wanna-Cry. We saw some attacks in North America and a couple in Europe. We had already patched for it.

What we are seeing is that we are in pretty good shape to screen out the run-of-the-mill stuff. It's the very sophisticated stuff that we have to worry about. It gets past your first line of defense, lands in an inbox, and somebody clicks on a link. Either Zscaler gets the link and blocks it, or our endpoint solution sees the unusual behavior and the device is quarantined until it can be cleaned up.

For a lot of companies, the cloud has complicated things. How do you extend your security fabric to multiple clouds? It's simple: just get a cloud cybersecurity service.

Before our transformation journey, we had a traditional 1970s hub-and-spoke design. Cisco helped us build a leaf-and-spine design—a fully meshed network between access switches and the backbone, many to many—using Cisco Unified Access Data Plane (UADP) switching ASICs. We spent all of 2017 building that. The design they helped us with is complete, and it is already implemented.

But we also recouped costs from all those remote offices that no longer needed the full stack of security appliances. It allowed us to invest in our future model.

Moving forward

It was rather hard to sell the transformation internally. I have been here two years. We were quite a traditional shop and we were happy building a moat around the data center and securing it. But when it comes to talking about different services, we could not build that ourselves, so we saw we needed to use public clouds. As we did research, people's attitudes came around. The biggest hurdle to overcome was around security.

I spent three days in Redmond at Microsoft doing a deep dive on the Azure architecture. When I came back, my boss asked what I thought of the security of Azure. I told him, "They are more secure than we are."

We had some savvy board members that encouraged me, and our first forays have been quite positive. We are proceeding with caution. We have an internal checklist for any app we plan to move to the cloud. If we believe there is a good business case, we will do it.

Large financial services are slow and steady. They are risk averse and heavily regulated. They are in the trust business. That comes with the responsibility to think very carefully about the fit of the cloud.

Lessons learned

The very first thing you have to do is take a temperature check of your internal culture. It is normal to be excited about moving things out to the cloud. Vendors will go directly to your internal people, bypassing any oversight you may have. If everyone says, "Yes move everything to the cloud," I would be equally worried. Ask yourself what is the primary driver. Is it security? Agility? Flexibility?

The ice that is under the water—that hidden infrastructure—is quite expensive. It is hard to find people with that knowledge of the architectural patterns.

"You have to communicate as you go through the journey. Celebrate success. Admit mistakes."

What not to do

- Try to prevent your internal business users from going directly to cloud suppliers themselves. They can punch a hole in your cyber fabric. They can enter into contracts that leave a nasty cost surprise. They can leave critical digital assets lying around. You have to be the cloud broker.

- Avoid moving things to the cloud simply because you don't like working with your internal IT people.

- If you move to the cloud and realize it was a mistake, acknowledge that and move it back.

CIO Journey | Great-West Life

Fannie Mae

Transforming Critical Financial Infrastructure
Behind the U.S. Economy

Company:	**Fannie Mae**	Revenue:	**$110 billion**
Sector:	**Financial Services**	Employees:	**7,200**
Driver:	**Bruce Lee**	Countries:	**1**
Role:	**CIO**	Locations:	**8**

Company IT Footprint: Fannie Mae has 10,000 people and over 10,000 servers in one or two data centers. They connect to about 2,500 banks and institutions, and to about 40 market providers of data or other types of services. They manage petabytes of data and 400 different applications. The complexity of its systems and infrastructure is not on the order of an international bank, but it is vital—it's systemically important.

"The point of this journey is to increase the resiliency
of the company."

Bruce Lee, Former Chief Information Officer, Fannie Mae

Fannie Mae is one of the major financial services organizations that underpins the economy of the United States. Bruce Lee, formerly the Chief Information Officer at Fannie Mae, describes the steps they took as they transformed their IT practices to a cloud model.

When we began our digital transformation journey here at Fannie Mae, we took a long hard look at what kind of company we were. We are a Fortune top 25 company with a three trillion dollar balance sheet and 14 billion dollars in profit.

I have been an IT person my whole career. I started off creating trading applications for banks in London. We were the disruptors back then, using PCs instead of mainframes. From there, my career has followed the disruptions in the financial space; in the derivatives world of interest rates and then foreign exchange. I was at HSBC until about 2012, when I got an opportunity at the New York Stock Exchange, and I thought, "Well if you really believe in technology's power to transform the market, we're witnessing that with high-speed trading." So I joined an industry in transition.

I came to Fannie Mae in 2014, when I saw that the mortgage market was transforming. The way that mortgages were created, serviced, and securitized was changing. The mortgage industry was probably the last of the financial services industries to get a real dose of technology transformation. In the past four years, we have been fundamentally rewriting the mortgage industry in the United States from our position as a secondary mortgage provider.

We have both the trading side and a B2B side to manage. The ecosystem is a big platform that does not look dissimilar to an Uber or Airbnb in that our job is to connect excess capacity—the world's financial capital—to excess

CIO Journey | Fannie Mae

demand. We just had to take that platform and renovate it. That's what we've been doing for the last few years.

At Fannie Mae, we are deemed part of the nation's critical financial infrastructure because we move so much money, we connect so many things. We have an outsized commercial impact, yet we are not that large in terms of people and servers. We manage petabytes of data and 400 different applications.

When it comes to starting down this path of digital transformation, I don't think CIOs spend enough time answering the questions: "Where are we today? Where do we want to be? And, how do we start the journey from here to there?"

When I joined, we had a lot of software development being done in the classical waterfall approach. We had five separate projects in which we were investing 100 million dollars a year, each. When you look at the track record of such large IT projects, you find there is a 96% failure rate, making them extraordinarily risky.

"I don't think CIOs spend enough time answering the questions: 'Where are we today? Where do we want to be? And, how do we start the journey from here to there?'"

We had a lot of departmental Sun boxes running Solaris, which meant a lot of application concentration onto individual servers. Most of our people were no longer programmers, but rather had become vendor managers because the development had been outsourced. We'd lost the core ability to engineer and architect. We'd become captive to our vendors in a very dysfunctional way.

That hard look was the start of our journey. While we found many areas we needed to improve, we found pockets of people who still have that imaginative view of what the future can be. I listened to them, as a new CIO must.

Defining a strategy

The main message was that we needed clarity of direction. We set out and made five bold statements about our IT strategy. One of them was that we would partner more closely with the business and make releases for structural applications every six months. This excited the agile team, but it scared the waterfall guys to death—but it also got everyone to a place in their heads where they said, "We've got to go faster."

Another goal of the new strategy was that we were going to embrace the cloud where it made sense. Stating that helped overcome the objections of the traditional IT forces internally.

A third objective was to build a team internally that could power our digital transformation by being core to the business. That means acquiring the skills, bringing in talent, pushing our vendors and outsourcers further away from us, and internalizing more of the work. This is a typical arc you will see in most agile digital transformations: you have to own more of the people yourself and you have to be more self-sufficient in software engineering and design. We have that as a goal.

We put another goal first that we called "fixing the foundations." That meant putting in place fundamental security and architectures that recognized how critical data was. At the end of the day, data is what matters most to us. Beyond cloud, beyond security, beyond everything. Who has that data? How accurate is it? And how can it be relied on? What intrinsic value does it have that a company like Fannie Mae can stand behind? These foundational improvements included partnering and agile delivery. It was adopting the cloud. It was sorting out the data and building the team to do it all.

Adopting SaaS

Moving to Salesforce led to interesting conversations with our business. The business wanted better Customer Relationship Management (CRM) tooling, but they were looking at it through what I call an old-world view. We pushed them to realize that they did not want a better tool for creating tickler notices to call a customer—what they really needed was a customer engagement tool. You want an environment where interested customers can find what they need on their own. You want to create a world that allows our own internal data view to intersect with the customer's view of themselves.

These conversations occurred when we were executing on our objective of IT partnering with the business. We evaluated other tools but ultimately went with Salesforce for CRM. We adopted Salesforce and immediately had to learn a valuable lesson, to learn to resist the temptation to over-customize SaaS tools—to try to make them fit our old way of thinking. We even had a group that redesigned the way the Salesforce interface worked until the end users asked, "Why does it scroll back and forth instead of up and down?" We learned to abandon that stuff and work with what Salesforce delivered.

Migrating internal applications

As we embraced the cloud more generally, we had to look at how to effectively move our own applications from our data centers to AWS. One of the challenges people have is that they underestimate a long-held core corporate tenet: that the infrastructure will be perfect, and applications can be written with that assumption. We will provide highly available clusters, and automatic disk mirroring, monitoring, and redundancy at the hypervisor level. We'll have transaction integrity maintained on the database backend, and the VMs will never go down. Because of that, application developers did not have to code resiliency into their applications.

In my experience, your approach to the cloud has to be that something can go wrong. VMs are easier to move around. They need to automatically recover. You have to worry about the state of your data and the multiple states it can be in. Basically, you have to think about all aspects of not having a perfect infrastructure. You can't rely on speed, for instance, as it will vary. In the internal corporate network, you spent a lot of time tuning everything to make sure that a transaction will never take more than 100 milliseconds. Because of that, you could guarantee what throughput would look like or know that two updates will be done close enough together and you won't have a data integrity problem.

With cloud, you can't take any of that for granted. You have to program for what it is and what happens if it slows down. The Intel updates for the Specter and Meltdown bugs that Amazon rolled out are a great example. Everything slowed down, and you had to adjust for that.

The interplay between hardware and software is much more loosely coupled in the cloud. That's what developers have to program for.

During 18 months of "test and learn", we tried to take a lot of corporate standards and design principles into AWS, and it was a disaster. We had to regroup after 18 months and implement a native cloud model rather than try to duplicate what we had in the data center.

We had anticipated this learning curve when we started, but we still had to go through it so people's hearts and minds would come over. They had to experience why it was difficult, why their paradigm doesn't work, and why they had to learn a new one.

I think of cloud migration for applications in the following ways. Corporate applications like HR systems and payroll systems should go to the cloud. Get the things that are not core to your business into the cloud. It's painful if it slows down, but it's not a problem. Then you have the other end of the spectrum, which is highly variable compute. Lots of compute, lots of data, but highly variable loads. That's another use case where you should definitely go to the cloud.

The challenge is the migration of your core transactional systems, your legacy Sun Solaris, Oracle transaction flows, the things that go up and down and are interlinked end to end across the whole company. There may be as many as 40 to 50 applications in a single business value chain. Decomposing that so the pieces can move to the cloud and be programmed in such a way that their variable performance does not impact your SLAs is the key. We are only now getting to see just how hard that is.

On top of creating a DevOps ecosystem, you have to figure out support. Your cloud infrastructure providers may not call you for two hours when they have a problem. In the meantime, you race around with your own troubleshooting only to discover the glitch was on their end.

Transforming the network and security infrastructures

When we started our cloud transformation, we performed a network hop analysis. This application spoke to this data set internally by making several hops. It would go from the application stack through two global load balancers and down to the storage arrays and find its data. It was a two- or three-hop technical journey from the view of the execution memory to the data we needed. When we put the same data set in AWS, because it was going to be used for analytics, we discovered we increased the number of network hops by a factor of three, to nine.

As you move applications to the cloud, you have to be aware of the network paths the data is going to take. You may leave your data where it is in the data center, but you have to be smart about all the hops it takes to get to it. You will invariably be adding layers and hops. You have to engineer that carefully. That may mean doubling down on the quality and depth of the networking team in your organization.

We embraced security as a journey that ran in parallel with our exploration of our applications, data, and transaction processing. We had phases of what we would allow along the journey and what we could support. And then we looked at what comes next, and what comes after that. We were fortunate in that the CISOs were of the mind to "make it work." We did not experience that typical battle with the security folks. They took the time to learn the AWS security stack, learn the way it works, and in many cases implement what was needed. We have assets in AWS, but we still connect back to our data centers and then out through our security stack before getting to the internet. The next step of our evolution is to put that security stack in Amazon, as well, to allow direct connections from inside Amazon to other places.

Establishing local breakouts

We are on the verge of pulling the trigger to allow our 10,000 employees to go directly to the internet from wherever they are. We use Zscaler Internet Access (ZIA) for that. The driver is Office 365. When you make that shift to Office 365, while still backhauling everyone's traffic to HQ, the bandwidth usage goes through the roof.

The point of this journey is to increase the resiliency of the company. Moving to Office 365 means that if we have issues with our systems, our employees can still get to email and SharePoint. Because of that, we went with Azure's hosted Active Directory, removing one more thing that could fail. If people cannot authenticate, they would not be able to get to Office 365.

Things to avoid

- Avoid saying it will be quick and easy to move to the cloud. It won't be. Just tell people it is much harder than they think.

- Try to avoid contention between developers and infrastructure people. Developers tend to jump to the cloud due to impatience with the controls in place. They don't want to wait for a server to be provisioned. They try to make the case that using the cloud is just easy.

We had to fight a lot of that at the beginning. It's natural for the developers to want to avoid working within the constraints of IT, but it always comes back to haunt you. Eventually, they have to interact with you, the security people, the data team, and network people. The myth that cloud is what drives developer productivity falls apart when you try to run anything in production for real; and run it at sustained levels; and have monitoring; and make sure it has the right backups; and that the resiliency is in place and that you've tested it; and the network doesn't get crowded out by something else.

To me, it means you are just shifting the pain to a different part of the organization: off the developers and onto their infrastructure colleagues. Developers, infrastructure, and security all have to be on the same page from the beginning.

There is no shortcut when you are building the hard stuff—the things that address real business and customer problems require integration across silos.

Things to do

- **The main point is to realize that your cloud migration journey, like your digital migration journey, is going to be multifaceted.** You should not think of it as one thing. You have your pure SaaS projects, your platforms like Salesforce and ServiceNow, and you have your office automation shelf like Office 365 and SharePoint. You can progress on one thing separate from the others. Moving Exchange to the cloud is a lot easier than moving a mortgage underwriting system to the cloud. One took nine months to organize, the other is going to take five years to complete.

- **Be precise in language usage.** Infrastructure as a service is different than platform as a service versus software as a service. They are all very different with different paths to success. Be especially careful with SharePoint. Customizations spread like wildfire and make it hard to migrate to the cloud. If I had to do it all over again I would have killed off SharePoint internally first.

- **The legal team has to adjust too.** They have to understand that the nature of the vendor-customer relationship has changed. They comb through contracts looking to customize them to the company's benefit. But cloud contracts are one size fits all. The provider cannot modify them for each customer. Which brings up an important insight I had.

Cloud introduces standards

A big "aha" moment for me was when I thought about the fact that we know intrinsically that systems—trade systems, cargo systems, any systems—all work better when you have standards. Think of railroads and standard gages. We know standards are good.

In corporate life, though, standards have become associated with avoiding the negative—security standards to prevent you from doing something stupid; database standards so you don't do anything stupid. They're seen as governance hurdles that limit creativity. Standards are somehow burdensome and bad. The beauty of the cloud is that it has managed to make standards sort of sexy, make them good things, because they free developers from the whole infrastructure nightmare. If your own infrastructure team tried to impose a whole bunch of standards on developers, they would hate it.

"The beauty of the cloud is that it has managed to make standards sort of sexy, make them good things, because they free developers from the whole infrastructure nightmare."

Developers are OK with just ticking boxes on AWS when they set up a VM. They don't think of them as standards; they don't fret over the fact that there are only three choices of configuration. They forget that they used to specify hundreds of different configurations on the corporate side, insisting that their application is special, it's different; they need this, they need that. In the cloud, they are perfectly happy with limited choices and just tick which ones they want.

Somehow the cloud has managed to make standards acceptable. The cloud is not customized, it is not bespoke. It's a very standard environment. I used to have 38 flavors of data replication in one data center at Fannie Mae; 38 ways that application teams had to decide their applications would move data from their primary system to their backup system. 38 of them. We had to close the data center to get down to ten ways, and now we have another big project underway to get that number down to two.

This move to standardization is a good thing for the industry.

PulteGroup

Building a Home in the Cloud

Company:	PulteGroup	Revenue:	**$7.6 billion**
Sector:	**Home Construction**	Employees:	**4,000**
Driver:	**Joe Drouin**	Countries:	**1**
Role:	**CIO**	Locations:	**700**

Company IT Footprint: Currently at Pulte, there are almost 5,000 employees. Pulte serves approximately 35 national markets across the United States, and have 600 to 700 active communities and 36 divisional offices around the country. Their IT footprint is around 5,000 desktop endpoints.

"If I were to advise a company in a similar position, I would say it helps to adopt a cloud-first mentality. Assume that everything is going to the cloud as a rule, and really challenge the exceptions. I don't think it's bold anymore; it's what you have to do today, and in my mind, it's proven."

Joe Drouin, Chief Information Officer, PulteGroup

Another cloud transformation story is from Joe Drouin, who is currently the Chief Information Officer at PulteGroup. He has overseen transformations at three separate companies: TRW, Kelly Services, and most recently the PulteGroup. Pulte is one of the largest home construction companies in the United States.

Evaluating our IT footprint

I'd been part of some fascinating IT transformations in the past, but this was certainly the most challenging. We had some legacy technology, systems, and applications that didn't support the business anymore. I was able to lean on my prior transformational experiences at TRW and Kelly to do the same kind of thing at Pulte.

In 2015 we started focusing on what we could do around our now 12-year-old application footprint. By 2016, we were ready to hit the accelerator. We spent all of 2017 laying out the roadmaps and our investment plans, building a fundamentally new architecture—a very cloud-centered architecture—and getting everything lined up for when the flow of investment kicked back in. As we entered 2018, we built out the underlying foundation and new architecture—our "enterprise data hub," a platform for integration that broke us out of our legacy environment of a point-to-point, 20-year-old, accidental architecture, to a more deliberate, modular, loosely coupled, API-centered one with a strong footprint in the cloud.

Pulte and the cloud

When I got to Pulte, everything was built on-premises. We had a data center in our office in Arizona. Almost everything was built or bought and housed in that data center. We had a traditional hub-and-spoke network with everything pointing back to that data center. Soon thereafter, we were running

CIO Journey | PulteGroup

out of space, were at capacity, and had to add space and power and cooling. The cloud was tried-and-true for me, having had much success with cloud platforms and SaaS at Kelly Services, so we started moving to it in earnest.

Beginning our cloud journey with Office 365 and local internet breakouts

We rolled out Office 365 and got off on-premises Exchange. Early on, we started purchasing SaaS solutions and slowly but surely moved more and more of our footprint out of the data center and into the cloud, which meant that we had to change the traditional hub-and-spoke model of the network. That's when we brought in Zscaler to help. I was familiar with Zscaler from my time at Kelly, and felt like Pulte was not a dissimilar model. We have lots of small locations that are constantly opening and closing.

"We started putting local internet into those locations, so we didn't have to backhaul all our traffic to the data center in Arizona"

We started putting local internet into those locations, so we didn't have to backhaul all our traffic to the data center in Arizona. Zscaler provided us the ability to do that and put all the security provisions in place that we needed. We moved more toward a hybrid design—we still sometimes have pipes back to the data center, but every location has connectivity via a local internet provider. This helped give us flexibility, but importantly it also reduced the delays we often experienced waiting for business-class service to be brought out to residential areas in far-flung suburbs, where often getting direct circuits took ages.

A hybrid cloud environment

As more and more of our capabilities are hosted in the cloud, it is important to be able to route traffic locally where it needs to go and back to the data center when needed. We still host our legacy ERP in the data center. We're currently deploying new and updated applications to Microsoft Azure. All our custom applications were built on .NET and SQL, so from the server OS to the database, all the way up through the development stack and to the desktop, we're a Microsoft environment. As such, Azure was a natural place for us to focus.

Costs will go up short term

There is an education process for IT and the whole business as you move into the cloud. One maybe not-so-obvious thing is there is often not a direct cost savings. During the transition stage, we are putting things in the cloud and paying by the drink but at the same time, we can't just turn the data center off. You can't shut down enough equipment in the data center fast enough to offset the cost of moving. Ultimately, the economics of it will pay off, but for a time we're carrying costs for our data center and we're incurring new costs. The idea of pay-per-use in the cloud is a great one. The idea that you can turn the dial up and down sounds great, though in my experience the dial only seems to go up.

End state: flexibility

I see us three or four years from now with a much more flexible IT environment, one that sits mainly in Microsoft's cloud but that would be containerized to the point that if we decided to spread the love a little and move some things out of Azure, it wouldn't be a problem. We will have this modular, plug-and-play architecture that will give us tremendous flexibility. In this

CIO Journey | PulteGroup

scenario, we will have applications that can be plucked out and replaced much more easily than trying to replace a big, monolithic, three-year software development project.

I think slowly but surely we will get to a point where there's very little on-premises technology. At the point we are ready to entertain the notion of replacing our finance system, I would certainly be looking for a cloud-based system.

Chapter 9 Takeaways

As the three CIOs in this chapter have shared, moving to the cloud has enabled them to move faster than they had previously imagined. It has brought their organizations flexibility and agility, and in some cases has allowed them to try things on a small scale before committing heavy resources or to prolonged timelines.

In summary, some key takeaways from these leaders are:

- Adopt a cloud-first mentality. Assume that everything is going to the cloud as a rule, and really challenge the exceptions. It's not bold anymore; it's what you have to do today, and it's proven.

- Ensure that the entire company is committed to the cloud-first strategy. This can be done incrementally by carving out projects that result in early wins. It can also be an all-in effort where top management recognizes the advantage of moving quickly, often driven by competitive pressures but also by customer demands.

- Plan application migration early. Create a blueprint for lift-and-shift, partial refactoring, and full refactoring of every application.

GETTING STARTED

Chapter 10: Creating Business Value

This chapter focuses on cloud economics and considerations for creating a compelling transformation business case when evaluating a migration to the cloud.

Chapter 11: Begin Your Transformation Journey

As you embark on the final chapter of this book, we'll leave you with a plan for beginning and evolving your transformation journey for a successful outcome.

Creating Business Value

―――――――――――――――――――――⌃―――――――――――――――――――――

""We moved 75 percent of our infrastructure to the cloud over about a three-year period for a savings of $100 million a year. We were then able to devote that savings back into things that mattered to our business."

Stephen Orban, General Manager, Amazon Web Services

―――――――――――――――――――――⌄―――――――――――――――――――――

The Power of Cloud Economics

One of the main drivers to cloud computing is the ability to right-size services and resources based on requirements and varying demands. In the cloud, enterprises pay for what they use and scale their investments with usage as their business needs evolve. Conversely, if demand decreases and capacity is no longer required, the cloud gives enterprises the ability to turn off systems, and they are not charged for underutilization. This model is vastly different than the traditional on-premises paradigm which was capital intensive as it required enterprises to pre-plan and procure additional capacity in anticipation of growth. In the pre-cloud world, IT organizations were also required to invest heavily in the day-to-day management and maintenance of their data centers and branches worldwide, placing tremendous pressures on enterprise CIOs to continue to innovate and grow, while grappling with the rising costs of IT.

Cloud transformation is disrupting both traditional and emerging business models and creating new opportunities for the enterprise. It is forcing IT to shift its mindset from being a service provider to a value broker, creating more efficient and cost-effective ways of conducting business to boost productivity and stay agile.

The move to the cloud often involves three transformation stages: application, network, and security transformation. When planning transformation steps and evaluating the financial investments and associated returns on those investments, it is important to note that application transformation savings can vary dramatically based on the type of applications being migrated or transformed. However, the cloud economics associated with network and security transformation is relatively straightforward to quantify. The rest of this chapter will focus on creating economic value for your business through network and security transformation.

Here are some data points that illustrate why legacy on-premises economics fails in this new world:

- A typical enterprise organization sees more than 50% of its WAN traffic destined for the internet, whether that's recreational or business usage, cloud, and SaaS. To add to that, the average compound annual growth rate (CAGR) for internet consumption is predicted to be 30% and you have traffic volumes that legacy network architectures were just not designed to handle.

- The cost of bandwidth is fast declining as internet usage on your network continues to increase exponentially. However, adding more bandwidth to offset legacy architecture limitations does little to address the escalating user performance concerns. Your legacy network topology and architecture has now become a bottleneck to delivering the very promise of cloud applications—improved productivity and enhanced user experiences.

If your WAN links are already predominantly carrying internet traffic and that traffic is anticipated to double in the next three years, are your WAN links really much more than expensive internet circuits? Moreover, aren't your data centers becoming just another hop to the cloud, where many of your applications now reside?

As we have learned through the experiences of many of the journeys in this book, this was typically the pivot point when they realized that the internet was becoming their new corporate network and the cloud, their new data center. This new dichotomy put them on a path to evaluate the options available and to carefully consider the technological, organizational, and financial imperatives of cloud transformation.

Evaluating your Transformation Costs

At this stage, you have probably begun the process of evaluating your cloud transformation options. What next? For the highest chance of success, your network transformation efforts should provide the most direct path to resources on the internet, and present immediate and long-term cost savings options. As we have highlighted in Chapter 4, to achieve this outcome you will need a cloud-native security service that allows you to leverage local internet breakouts while removing the cost, complexity, and risks associated with deploying local security at each branch. With this strategy, you will be able to transform as many branches as your organization needs through your cloud journey while providing your employees at every branch with the required security capabilities and superior user experience, all the while helping keep your future costs flat.

In prior chapters, we've also highlighted that the focus of the new model is the user and not the number of locations you need to support. In this new model, you now have the power to migrate branches and users away from centralized gateways based on the priorities you define, and without incurring additional costs or changes in policy and security.

Expecting a 30% increase in internet traffic requires IT teams to plan regular upgrades to meet this change in demand. These upgrades usually encompass three key components: security appliances, internet (ISP) bandwidth, and WAN bandwidth. Planning for growth in these areas is nothing new to IT professionals as they have regularly had to plan for regular increases in traffic. The significant difference between today and five years ago is just how critical the role of the internet has become in day-to-day business. Planning for scheduled cutovers or holding off on necessary upgrades could be materially disruptive to the business.

Properly planned and executed, your secure cloud transformation eliminates the need to upgrade all three components. Here's how:

Security Appliances

Transformation with a cloud security architecture mitigates the need to scale appliance footprints and, in many cases, eliminates the need for appliances completely. Appliances are sized around throughput, and the only way to scale is to add boxes or by refreshing to higher capacity boxes sooner. Unless your current appliances are running at only 20% utilization, which is highly unlikely, you are looking at increasing your capacity in the next two to three years. This applies to every inline security appliance in your stack: IPS, firewalls, proxy, SSL decryption, and so on. With local internet breakouts, you're diverting traffic away from large internet gateways to your cloud security service. In this new paradigm, scale is no longer a problem, and there is no need to plan for upgrades to your security appliances, resulting in a straightforward future-cost avoidance win.

Once you've broken out branches, you can retire your internet gateway appliances, in favor of a single admin console. That means eliminating your annual OPEX spend on hosting facilities, vendor maintenance, licensing, and support, and eliminating the CAPEX required to purchase and refresh hardware. It also helps avoid the need to hire experts to support the latest security capabilities your company needs to remain secure in this ever-changing threat landscape.

Internet Bandwidth

As the majority of your users become mobile and the applications they utilize move to the cloud, and as more and more of your traffic becomes internet-bound, the next logical step is to move your security and controls to the cloud as well. By implementing bandwidth management, you can enforce application prioritization policies in the cloud across your organization from a single console, without any hardware or software to deploy or manage, eliminating bottlenecks and reducing costs associated with traditional solutions.

WAN Bandwidth

As we've previously discussed, network transformation helps you control and remove costs incurred as a result of backhauling internet traffic across the WAN from the branches. A 30% impending annual increase in internet traffic affects all lines of connectivity between users and their destinations. Therefore, if a user is traveling across a WAN link to the data center for egress, that WAN link is subject to the same 30% CAGR. It is helpful at this stage to analyze how much of your WAN traffic is internet bound and ascertain when and which upgrades should be considered.

If you are considering a hybrid network with both MPLS and ISP connectivity at the branches, you can eliminate the need for future MPLS circuit upgrades because you will no longer be backhauling the internet traffic that impacts your WAN demand growth. As your applications and services move from your data centers to the cloud, there is less traffic traversing to and from the data center. Your MPLS costs can stay flat or be reduced. For organizations considering an internet-only approach for some branches, MPLS can be eliminated in favor of low-cost internet connections. Through network transformation, you can avoid the need to upgrade your existing WAN circuits and reduce the required bandwidth of WAN circuits as a result of off-loading internet traffic to local ISP circuits.

Business Value Justification

Let's turn to a value creation model to quantify the positive economic benefits of secure cloud transformation. The methodology and output should help you derive the business value justifications required to navigate through the steps of your transformation journey.

This model was constructed to represent a typical network transformation project for an enterprise organization with 5,000 users at 50 branch locations. The model assumes that, before the completion of the branch transformation project, all branches backhaul internet traffic to one of six regional or centralized data centers. Each data center in the model has an internet egress gateway consisting of four web security appliances, four SSL inspection appliances, and two internal next-generation firewalls. Also, the model estimates an average WAN connectivity cost of USD $2,400 per month for each branch.

Summary of value creation model assumptions:

- 5,000 users
- 50 branch locations
- Average WAN cost of USD $2,400 per month per branch (20mbps)
- All branches backhaul internet traffic to one of 6 data centers
- The six data center gateways include (in total):
  - 24 web security appliances (USD $432K annual)
  - 24 SSL inspection appliances (USD $324K annual)
  - 12 internal next-generation firewalls (USD $108K annual)
  - Hosting costs (USD $60K annual)
- 50% of WAN traffic is going to the internet
- Internet consumption is growing at an annual rate of 30% (CAGR)
- Cost of internet connectivity 15% relative to the cost of MPLS
- Network transformation project is complete
- This example covers hard costs only—vendor-specific investment costs are not included

Based on the value assessment model, here's an example of how your organization could benefit from cloud transformation.

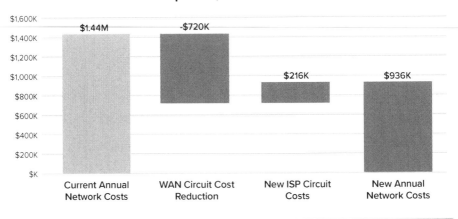

Figure 10.1 Year 1 net impact as a result of transformation

Figure 10.1 illustrates how the current-state hard costs are reduced by replacing traditional WAN circuits with lower-cost internet circuits that provide more available bandwidth. The starting point of USD $1.44M annual run rate of WAN costs is reduced by USD $720K through the MPLS circuit reductions. The additional USD $216K cost for internet connections results in a net impact of USD $504K per year, lowering the overall run rate to USD $936K (a 35% reduction in costs).

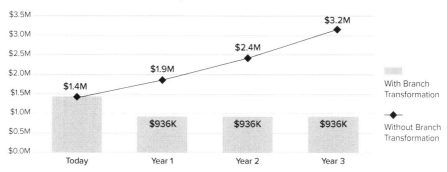

3-Year Projected Future WAN Costs

Branch Transformation Cost Reduction

Annual Net WAN Cost Reduction with Breakouts Instead of Backhauling Traffic	**$504K**
Annual WAN Cost Avoidance with 30% CAGR Applied	**$1.05M**
3-Year Cumulative Savings	**$4.66M**

Figure 10.2 Three-year WAN cost projection comparing costs as-is vs. cost savings from branch network transformation.

Without branch transformation, the existing WAN circuits are subject to 30% compound annual growth rates as a result of increased internet demand from further adoption of cloud and SaaS. However, with branch transformation, the benefits realized in the first full year post-network transformation alone will carry over year-over-year. Implementing additional capabilities such as bandwidth control can help mitigate the 30% CAGR. This results in a USD $2.23M delta three years out, and a three-year cumulative savings of $4.66M or 62% of what would otherwise have been spent over those three years if not for transformation, as illustrated in Figure 10.2.

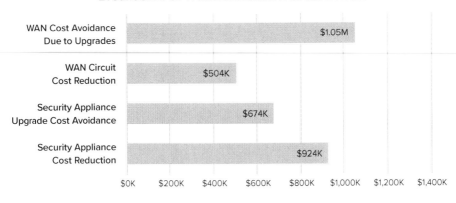

Breakdown of Transformation Benefit Drivers

WAN Cost Avoidance Due to Upgrades	$1.05M
WAN Circuit Cost Reduction	$504K
Security Appliance Upgrade Cost Avoidance	$674K
Security Appliance Cost Reduction	$924K

$0K $200K $400K $600K $800K $1,000K $1,200K $1,400K

Figure 10.3 Annual cost benefits breakdown of network and security transformation (over 3 years)

On the network side, future WAN costs can be avoided by mitigating the 30% internet consumption CAGR and through the reduction of current WAN costs by eliminating backhaul as seen in Figure 10.3. With security transformation the same 30% internet consumption CAGR that would normally require in-place upgrades or more frequent hardware refreshes can be avoided, while existing security appliances are displaced through simplification in the cloud.

In this model, security transformation removes 24 web proxy appliances, 24 SSL inspection appliances, and 12 outbound firewalls across the six data centers. The removed hard costs include hardware (annualized capital expenditure depreciation), software, licensing, and annual vendor maintenance. Soft costs that would include contractor and device management costs associated with managing the legacy security infrastructure such as incident management, break/fix, and so on, are not factored in this model due to the considerable variability of these costs from scenario to scenario.

Chapter 10 Takeaways

- Secure cloud transformation creates business value by both driving top line growth and improving the bottom line.

- In addition to enabling cloud transformation, network transformation yields significant cost savings of its own, making you not only an enabler of business outcomes but also a hero to the bottom line.

- Engaging in a comprehensive business value analysis early on in the process helps to map the organization's business goals to the benefits cloud transformation offers. It also provides a structured approach for evaluating all the considerations that accompany a move to the cloud.

- A value creation framework helps organizations better understand the impact of their cloud transformation journey across multiple dimensions. Such a framework can also identify secondary benefits that exist beyond the immediate IT impact, e.g., any hidden on-premises hardware costs, factor in the impact of highly variable soft costs such as personnel and management costs that are typically not incorporated into a hard cost TCO model.

- A value creation analysis can also help the company set a timetable for transformation and identify options and steps to derive cost savings as well as cost avoidance.

CHAPTER 11

Begin Your Transformation Journey

"When it comes to moving a large organization, cloud transformation is 70% cultural and 30% technical."

Philip Armstrong, Chief Information Officer, Great-West Life

There is an old Chinese proverb that states, "The best time to plant a tree was twenty years ago. The second best time is today." Cloud transformation has become imperative for any organization that wants to not only survive in a changing world but wants to thrive. An IT leader may have reservations about cloud transformation based on two primary concerns: Can cloud transformation happen without making disastrous mistakes? And can it be done securely? The answer to both questions is "yes" and here are some best practices as gleaned from many of the IT leaders in this book on how to accomplish a seamless and successful cloud transformation for your enterprise.

Overcome resistance

A decision to start down the cloud path is often prone to resistance. The level of resistance to change varies from organization to organization—people are comfortable with what they have been doing, and how they have been doing it. The technology, network configurations, applications, and data centers that have been purchased or built at great expense are still functioning today. Why disrupt that?

The cloud brings about a dramatic change that entails giving up the physical control of servers, hiring new talent, training developers and IT support staff in new technologies, and getting an organization to work together towards a new mandate. The sunk cost in security gear and multiple layers of alerting and reporting tools will be written off. But, as can be seen from the many stories from the IT leaders featured in this book who have successfully navigated their cloud transformations, the benefits are real and multifold.

Cost savings, agility, better security, and new capabilities can all help drive that decision. Some of the IT leaders in this book took an all-in approach, while others took an incremental path.

Make a plan

Evaluate the business areas or applications where cloud adoption can have the most immediate impact. Convene a team of stakeholders including your architects, security team, finance, and senior management. Get a snapshot of where the company stands today versus where it has to go from a technology perspective. Is there a need to modernize, similar to what Philip Armstrong at Great-West Life shares in Chapter 9? Do your customers expect more of you? Have you had a breach recently? Did NotPetya or WannaCry impact your operations? Are you having trouble staffing your DevOps, security, and IT leadership roles? Do you have the right people, partners ,and technology to embark on the phases of this transformation journey?

Map your network and future plans for new locations. Quantify the amount you spend on MPLS circuits. Have you budgeted for a gateway refresh to upgrade your firewalls? Do you understand what your traffic mix is—internal versus external? How much of your traffic is encrypted?

How did your last M&A experience fare? Could you quickly consolidate IT operations or is that still ongoing? Will there be any future M&A activities?

Considerations before you begin

As you embark on your cloud journey keep these four things in mind:

Finding the budget

Alex Philips at NOV used cloud transformation as a cost savings measure. A downturn in the oil and gas industry created an immediate requirement for his organization to reduce costs. He discovered that he could provide more services at a higher quality and with less budget. For others there may have been a need for additional budget, especially when launching cloud projects in parallel with legacy approaches, with a plan to switch over later. Demonstrate to your team and superiors how future savings from getting out of the data center business will provide your organization with a return on that investment.

Get your team onboard

Perhaps the greatest challenge to a successful cloud transformation is changing the mindset of your team. This starts with top leadership—you need to create champions and supporters. They have to be convinced that moving to the cloud is the right decision for your organization, and they have to communicate that conviction clearly.

Overcoming this hurdle starts with having the right team to execute on this journey. You may have to hire new talent or bring in an experienced team of consultants. One CIO (not interviewed for this book) took a dictatorial approach. He convened a meeting of his IT staff to announce their cloud-first strategy. He informed them that if anyone who was not happy with this new direction should quite simply "pack up and go hug their server goodbye." That may be the right approach at some organizations to get change to happen, but more the exception than the norm. Most leaders will find that winning the hearts and the minds of their teams will be more productive.

Start by creating a simple and clear message that can serve as a mantra for the organization. Offer training in cloud services to your developers. By now most developers understand that career advancement comes with being cloud savvy. A firewall administrator may wonder what will happen to his or her job if there are no more firewalls. Fortunately, there are always valuable roles for security and network people. They can be engaged to ensure that applications get refactored securely. They can spend more time on red/blue team exercises. The mundane day-to-day tasks of upgrading and patching the firewall policy change control can now be replaced with strategic decisions and activities that put them on the frontline of cyber defense for the organization.

Select the right cloud service provider for your business needs

Your planning exercise should aim to lay out the requirements for the technology stack. Understand what is required from your SaaS services. For application transformation, prioritize which internal applications need to be moved to the cloud. For network transformation, prioritize meeting with your telecom provider and learn who they partner with. Learn what technology has worked for companies of a similar size and geographic distribution. Be aware of the technology interdependencies in your network and security stacks.

One aspect of ROI that is hard to measure is the cost savings from avoiding security incidents. If you have historical data on the time and costs associated with out-of-cycle patches, the clean-up of infected hosts, password changes to compromised accounts, and recovery from ransomware, you will be well armed to claim those cost savings for your return on investment calculations.

How to de-risk cloud transformation

One of the attractions of the cloud is that technology decisions and innovation in the cloud are inherently less risky than with legacy models. Gone are the days where switching ERP vendors or computing platforms were multi-year projects. Where once there were long-term risks and costs associated with making technology decisions, the cloud introduces agility and flexibility. We are not advocating that it is always pain-free to switch from one SaaS application to another or one public cloud to another, but it is much easier than the retrofit of equipment and data centers that these types of decisions called for in the past.

De-risk your cloud transformation by picking partners that use open standards and integrate with the other major players. Avoid taking steps that lock you into a particular supplier. Evaluate if you can move your applications across clouds—Azure to AWS to Google Cloud. If you are doing network transformation with SD-WAN, ensure that your SD-WAN investment will work with multiple telecom providers and that you can decouple your identity and access management solution from the rest of your technology stack.

Build justification for investment

The importance of measurement comes into play when you are demonstrating return on investment. If you are considering network and security transformation, make sure that the cost savings from eliminating MPLS charges and avoiding the refresh of network security gear every three years is tracked. In this way you can build support for your cloud transformation efforts. While your costs go down, your users, like those at National Oilwell Varco as highlighted in Chapter 5, will think you are spending more as they notice consistent response times from wherever they are located. They will get access to new features in applications as they come out. Performance of key apps like Office 365 will improve. No more cumbersome VPNs to deal with from hotels and airplanes.

How to begin

The cloud journey begins with identity.

The first step to cloud migration is to get identity right. Choose an identity management system that:

1. Holds all the identities of your employees and contractors

2. Integrates with multiple authentication systems (username/password, one-time password tokens, biometrics, card keys)

3. Provides granular control over authorizations by individual and group

4. Is standards-based

The key is to consolidate identity to a single provider. In the cloud world, this is often Azure Active Directory, Okta, or Ping. Have one identity for the enterprise. This is not an easy task, but it is the most critical step in getting your cloud transformation right.

Start with SaaS applications

As Scott Guthrie from Microsoft shared in Chapter 7, the best place to start your cloud journey is with SaaS. You immediately begin to experience the benefits of the cloud. Most companies start with Salesforce or Microsoft Dynamics for a CRM package, or Workday for HR, or ServiceNow for customer support. If you have a significant investment in a software application in your data center for one of these capabilities, perform a Total Cost of Ownership (TCO) analysis to see if continuing to maintain on-premises software is the best thing. Audit which custom features your team has developed over the years, and ascertain if they can be replaced by an SaaS product. Every in-house application you transition to SaaS is one less headache for maintenance and support and frees up resources for the next phase.

And then there is Office 365, which is on the radar of every large enterprise. But this requires careful planning for a successful deployment because it can be a burden to the network, has a lot of moving parts, and touches every employee.

Use public cloud for other applications

Identify your most critical business applications for which there isn't a viable SaaS replacement. Start to refactor your applications so they can run in the public cloud. This exercise could be as straightforward as moving them from your data center to the cloud (lift and shift). You may have to "webify" the user interface or change the backend database (partial refactoring). Look at applications that have to be rewritten entirely (refactored). This is your chance to make the application fit for purpose, or expose it to more users, or even to customers.

Move to a hybrid network

Once the move to SaaS and public cloud is underway, take a look at your network usage. You will find that much of your traffic is being backhauled from remote locations just to be re-routed to the internet. Improve the user experience at those locations by providing local internet breakout as Siemens did [see Chapter 3]. Their web browsing experience will be dramatically improved, and the corporate network will no longer be a bottleneck to their productivity.

Deploying local breakouts is your chance to capture cost savings. Local breakouts enable you to downsize your expensive MPLS circuits or eliminate them altogether.

Securely connect your users to applications

As you move closer and closer to a network topology that uses the internet as your corporate network, you can progress to a cloud security model. Security and access controls are as close to the users as possible within each office, and every user connects first to a cloud security checkpost over an encrypted link. The checkpost replaces your gateway security devices, and delivers cost savings. And like other cloud services, the tasks of managing updates, configurations, and patching now is handled by your cloud security provider, relieving you of the operational overhead. A good example of this is shared by Ken Athanasiou of AutoNation in Chapter 4.

All your traffic should be over SSL to provide for secure communications. Ensure that your security solution gives you the capability to inspect SSL traffic.

To complete your cloud transformation securely, ensure secure access to all your internal applications regardless of user or device location, be it on the manufacturing plant floor, ERP systems, or IoT devices in the field. Use a cloud security checkpost to broker connections between authenticated users and the applications they are authorized to use. These internal applications now become invisible to the outside world. Only your users will be able to find them, whether they are in your data center or hosted in the public cloud. Tony Fergusson of MAN Energy shares a good example of this in Chapter 4.

Begin Your Journey

The best time to start your cloud journey is today. Use these steps to create a future where the cloud is your data center and the internet is your corporate network. It is a future where users can access the applications they need from anywhere in the world, securely.

APPENDIX

Contributor Bios

Index

About the Author

Contributor Bios

Philip Armstrong
EVP and CIO Great-West Life

Philip joined Great-West Life in January of 2016 and is currently responsible for all technology strategy, delivery, infrastructure, procurement, and operations, with a focus on technology architecture, cyber security, digital transformation, hybrid-cloud enablement, employee productivity, big data analytics, A.I., and robotic process automation. Reporting to the CEO, Philip is a member of the Executive Management Committee. Prior to joining Great-West Life, Philip held global roles as the Chief Digital Technology Officer for Sun Life Financial and the Chief Technology Officer for Manulife Financial/John Hancock. Philip holds a Bachelor of Administrative Studies from York University and a BTEC from Leeds University (Keighley College).

Ken Athanasiou
VP and CISO, AutoNation; Founding board member of Retail Cyber Intelligence Sharing Center; Former CISO, American Eagle Outfitters

Ken Athanasiou oversees AutoNation's information security functions. He has extensive experience in data security, data risk management, and the resolution of security problems. His career spans 23 years and includes senior positions with companies in the retail, banking, and financial service sectors as well as seven years of service in the United States Air Force.

Athanasiou earned a bachelor's degree in computer information systems from Park University and a master's degree in computer resources management from Webster University. He was a member of the Honor Flight at the USAF Officer Training School and holds CISSP certification.

Larry Biagini
Technology Evangelist and Adviser; Former VP and CTO, General Electric Company

Larry Biagini recently retired as Vice President and Chief Technology Officer of GE. While at GE, Larry's focus was on upgrading infrastructure, employee services, and deploying cloud technology enabling secure usage of those services by GE's employees, customers, and partners.

In his twenty-six years at GE, Larry held various positions in Information Technology including Vice President of IT Risk, having responsibility for all aspects of risk, governance, and security; Vice President & CIO, GE Capital; Chief Technology Officer, CIO & Services Delivery for GE; and Chief Technology Officer for GE Aviation. During his tenure at GE, Larry was instrumental in driving successful technology integrations of global mergers, acquisitions, and divestitures. In 2012 Larry was named a GE Company Officer. Larry holds a Bachelor of Science in Accounting from Fairfield University.

Hervé Coureil
Chief Digital Officer, Schneider Electric

Hervé Coureil joined Schneider Electric in 1993 and has been the Chief Digital Officer since June 2017. Prior to assuming this role, Hervé served as CIO and was responsible for information technology, processes, and organization globally. Previously he was the CFO for the Critical Power and Cooling Services Business Unit of Schneider Electric. Hervé's responsibilities included overseeing legal, IT, and strategy. Hervé holds a master's degree in management from Reims Management School and is a graduado en Ciencias Empresariales Europeas from ICADE in Madrid.

Joe Drouin
CIO, PulteGroup

Joe Drouin is vice president and chief information officer for PulteGroup Inc., one of the nation's largest homebuilders. In his role, Joe leads all aspects of information technology for the company and is based at the company's headquarters in Atlanta, GA. Prior to joining Pulte, Joe was SVP & CIO for Kelly Services, Inc. in Troy, MI, where he also ran the company's global service organization. Before joining Kelly, Joe was chief information officer at TRW Automotive Holdings, where he also led a team responsible for global supply chain logistics. Joe's background includes substantial international experience, including a number of years living and working in Asia and Europe. Joe earned an MBA from the University of Western Ontario and holds a bachelor's degree in management information systems from the University of Memphis.

Tony Fergusson
IT Infrastructure Architect, MAN Energy Solutions

Tony Fergusson is an Infrastructure Architect, working with many technologies within the enterprise with a focus on security. Tony has over 20 years of experience in the IT industry and has been recently focusing his efforts on how to secure the enterprise and the Internet of Things using emerging technologies like software defined networking and cloud security. Tony is also the former Senior System Engineer at OneNet. He earned his Bachelor of Engineering degree in Software and Electronic Engineering from the Central Institute of Technology in 1995.

Jim Fowler
Former Group CIO, General Electric Company

Jim Fowler is Executive Vice President and Chief Information Officer of Nationwide. In this role, he is responsible for the company's technology strategy, IT capabilities, and business transformation programs. Prior to joining Nationwide in 2018, Jim was Chief Information Officer for General Electric, where he led the company's global information technology strategy, services, operations, and internal digital transformation program. Prior to his 18-year career at GE, he held IT roles with NCR and Accenture. Jim holds a Bachelor of Science degree in Management Information Systems and Marketing from Miami University, and a Master of Business Administration degree from Xavier University. He is also a certified Six Sigma Black Belt. Jim serves on the Information Systems Advisory Board at Miami University and as a national board member for Year Up. He is well recognized for his results-oriented leadership style and his ability to drive innovation,and was recently recognized by Forbes with the CIO Innovation Award.

Scott Guthrie
EVP, Cloud and Enterprise Group, Microsoft

Scott Guthrie is best known for his work on ASP.NET, which he and colleague Mark Anders developed while at Microsoft. He runs the Microsoft Azure team as well as the development teams that build Windows Server, Microsoft SQL Server, Active Directory, System Center, Visual Studio, and .NET. Guthrie graduated with a degree in computer science from Duke University. He joined Microsoft in 1997.

Frederik Janssen
Global Head of Service Portfolio & Lifecycle Management, IT Infrastructure, Siemens

Over an 18-year career, Frederik served nine years in various roles focused on software development, software engineering, software architecture, data-base systems, database development, and web application before becoming Head of Corporate Governance for IT Infrastructure at Siemens in 2012. He has held his current role as Global Head of Service Portfolio & Lifecycle Management, IT Infrastructure, since 2014. He studied computer science at Steinbeis-Hochschule-Berlin.

Erik Klein
Infrastructure Architect, FrieslandCampina

Erik is an ICT Telecommunications Manager and Infrastructure Architect with extensive experience in Telecommunications Strategy and ITT/RFP program management and vendor management on a global scale. His career has spanned 25 years in the IT industry, with almost 14 years at Jones Lang LaSalle and 6 years at FrieslandCampina in different roles. His areas of focus include: designing and implementing a phased approach to zero-trust networks, the effect of Bring Your Own Device (BYOD) on enterprise security and compliance, and architecting and designing a new global SD-WAN environment for FrieslandCampina.

Bruce Lee
Former CIO, Fannie Mae; current SVP and head of Technology Infrastructure and Operations, Centene Corporation

Bruce is an expert CIO/COO, having run and transformed some of the country's most critical financial systems' infrastructure and operations. He is focused on creating the skills and culture needed to ensure Tech and Ops can support corporate strategy execution in the world of digital disruption and transformation.

Stephen Orban
General Manager, Amazon Web Services; author of *Ahead in the Cloud: Best Practices for Navigating the Future of Enterprise IT*

Stephen spent his first three and a half years with Amazon as the Global Head of Enterprise Strategy, where he oversaw AWS's enterprise go-to-market strategy, and invented and built AWS's Migration Acceleration Program (MAP).

Prior to joining AWS, Stephen was the CIO of Dow Jones, where he introduced modern software development methodologies and reduced costs while implementing a cloud-first strategy. Stephen also spent 11 years at Bloomberg LP, holding a variety of leadership positions across their equity and messaging platforms, before founding Bloomberg Sports in 2008, where he served as CTO.

Stephen earned his bachelor's degree in computer science from State University of New York College at Fredonia.

Alex Philips
CIO, National Oilwell Varco

Alex Philips is the Chief Information Officer of National Oilwell Varco (NOV). In this position, Alex is responsible for overseeing all aspects of Information Technologies, Systems, Applications, and Security to further strategic goals. Alex joined Phoenix Energy Services, now a part of National Oilwell Varco, in 1997 as an IT Network Administrator. During Alex's 17-year tenure at NOV he has served in various roles including IT Infrastructure Manager, ERP Director and, most recently, Chief Information Security Officer. Alex is a graduate of Rice University with a Master of Business Administration.

Jim Reavis
Co-founder and CEO, Cloud Security Alliance

Jim has worked in the information security industry as an entrepreneur, writer, speaker, technologist, and business strategist. His innovative ideas about emerging security trends are widely published and presented. In 1998, he founded SecurityPortal, then the largest information security website. As the Cloud Security Alliance's cofounder and CEO, he is shaping the future of information security and technology industries. He received a BA in business administration and computer science from Washington University, where he serves on the alumni board.

Tariq Shaukat
President, Partner and Industry Platforms, Google Cloud

Before joining Google, Tariq was Chief Commercial Officer of Caesars Entertainment Corporation since October 2014 and its Executive Vice President since March 2012. Tariq served as Chief Marketing Officer of Caesars Entertainment Corporation from March 2012 to October 2014. Prior to this, Tariq was a Principal at McKinsey & Company from July 2009 to March 2012. He also served as Engagement Manager from 2005 to 2007 and as Associate Principal from 2007 to 2009. He earned his BS in Mechanical Engineering and MS in Technology and Policy from MIT, and a master's in Mechanical Engineering from Stanford University.

Darryl Staskowski
SVP and CIO, Kelly Services

As CIO, Darryl oversees the implementation of innovative solutions and is responsible for all aspects of information technology, information security, data, and analytics across the global organization. Prior to Kelly Services, Darryl was a Director of IT operations for TRW Automotive's global manufacturing plants. He earned his BS in Computer Science, Mathematics, from Western Michigan University.

Index

About the Author

 Richard Stiennon is Chief Research Analyst for IT-Harvest, the firm he founded in 2005 to cover the 2,200 vendors that make up the IT security industry. He has presented on the topic of cybersecurity in 29 countries on six continents. He is a lecturer at Charles Sturt University in Australia. He is the author of *Surviving Cyberwar* (Government Institutes, 2010) and Washington Post Best Seller, *There Will Be Cyberwar*. He writes for *Forbes*, *CSO Magazine*, and *The Analyst Syndicate*. He is a member of the advisory board at the Information Governance Initiative and sits on the Responsible Recycling Technical Advisory Board, the standard for electronic waste. In previous roles Stiennon was Chief Strategy Officer for Blancco Technology Group, the Chief Marketing Officer for Fortinet, Inc. and VP Threat Research at Webroot Software. Prior to that he was VP Research at Gartner, Inc. He has a B.S. in Aerospace Engineering and his MA in War in the Modern World from King's College, London.